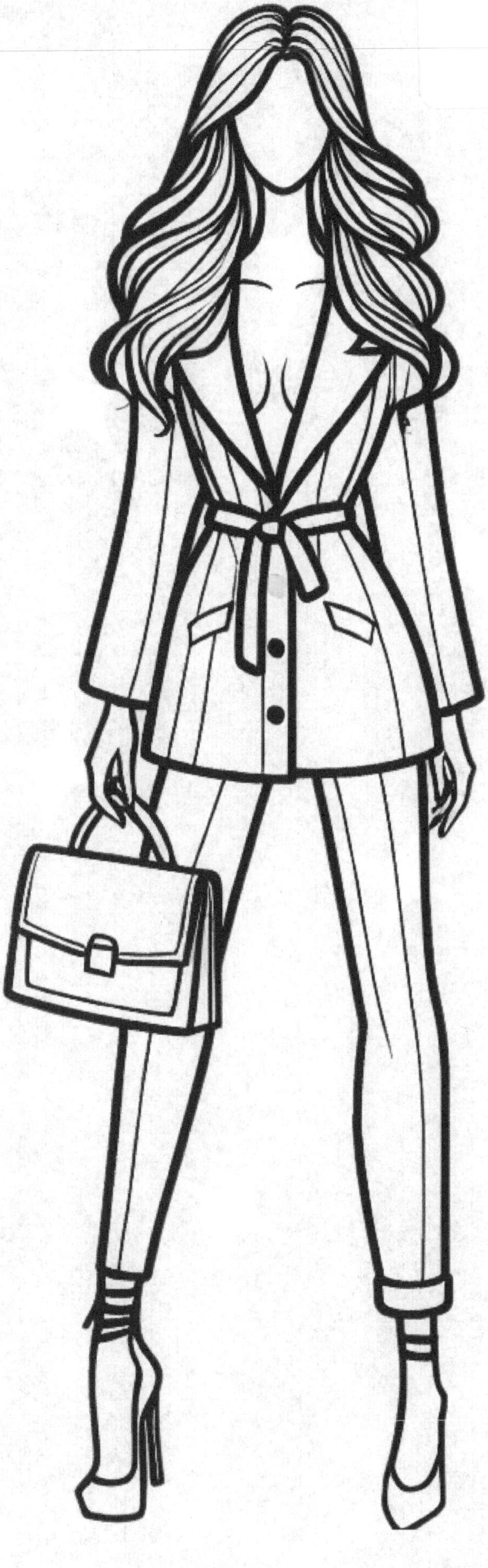

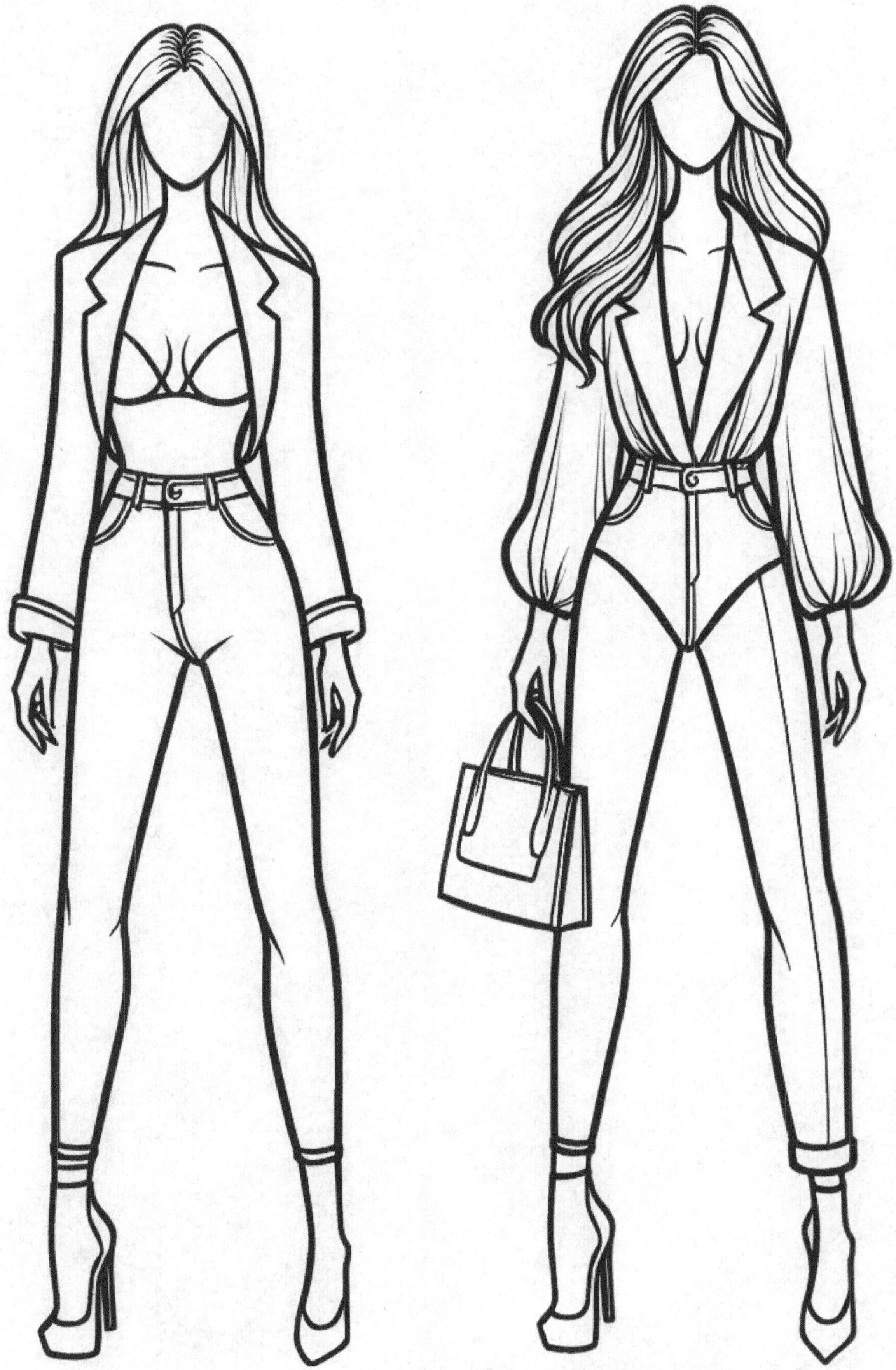

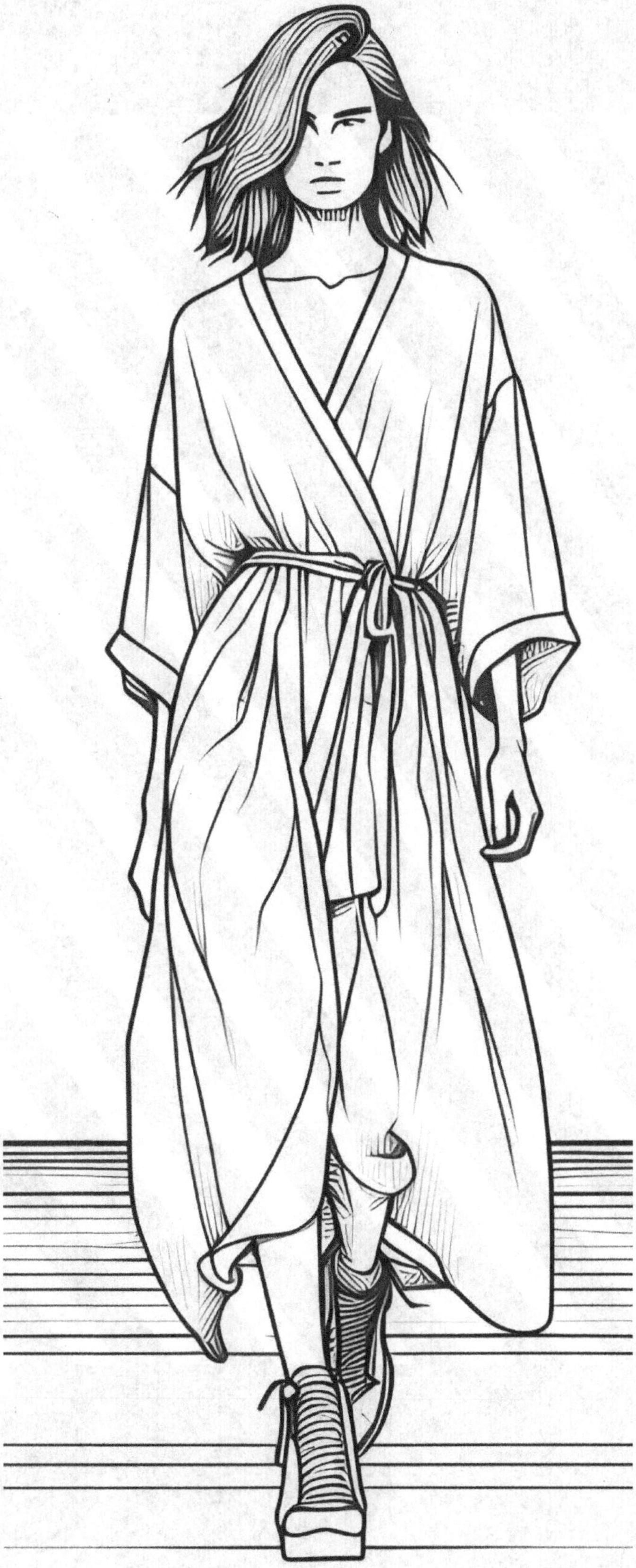

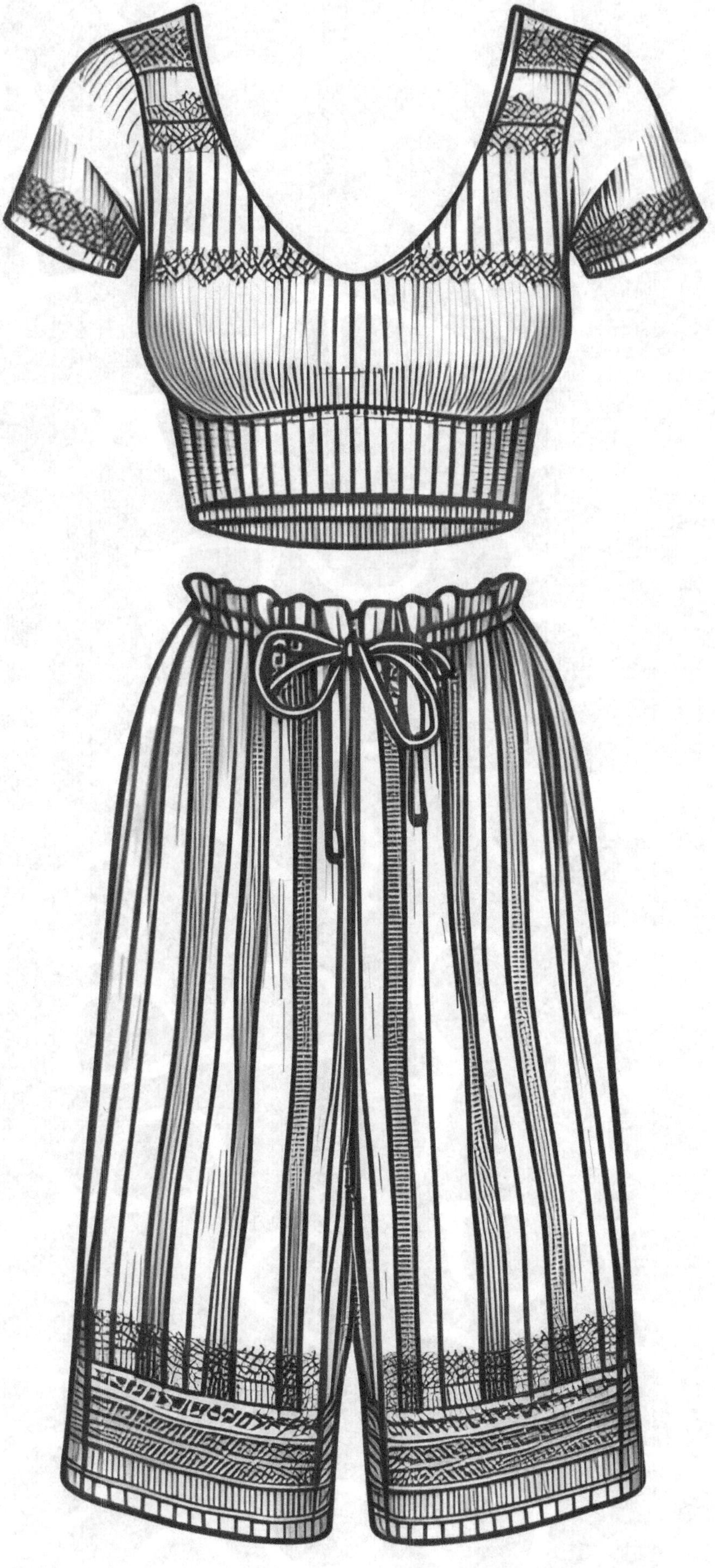

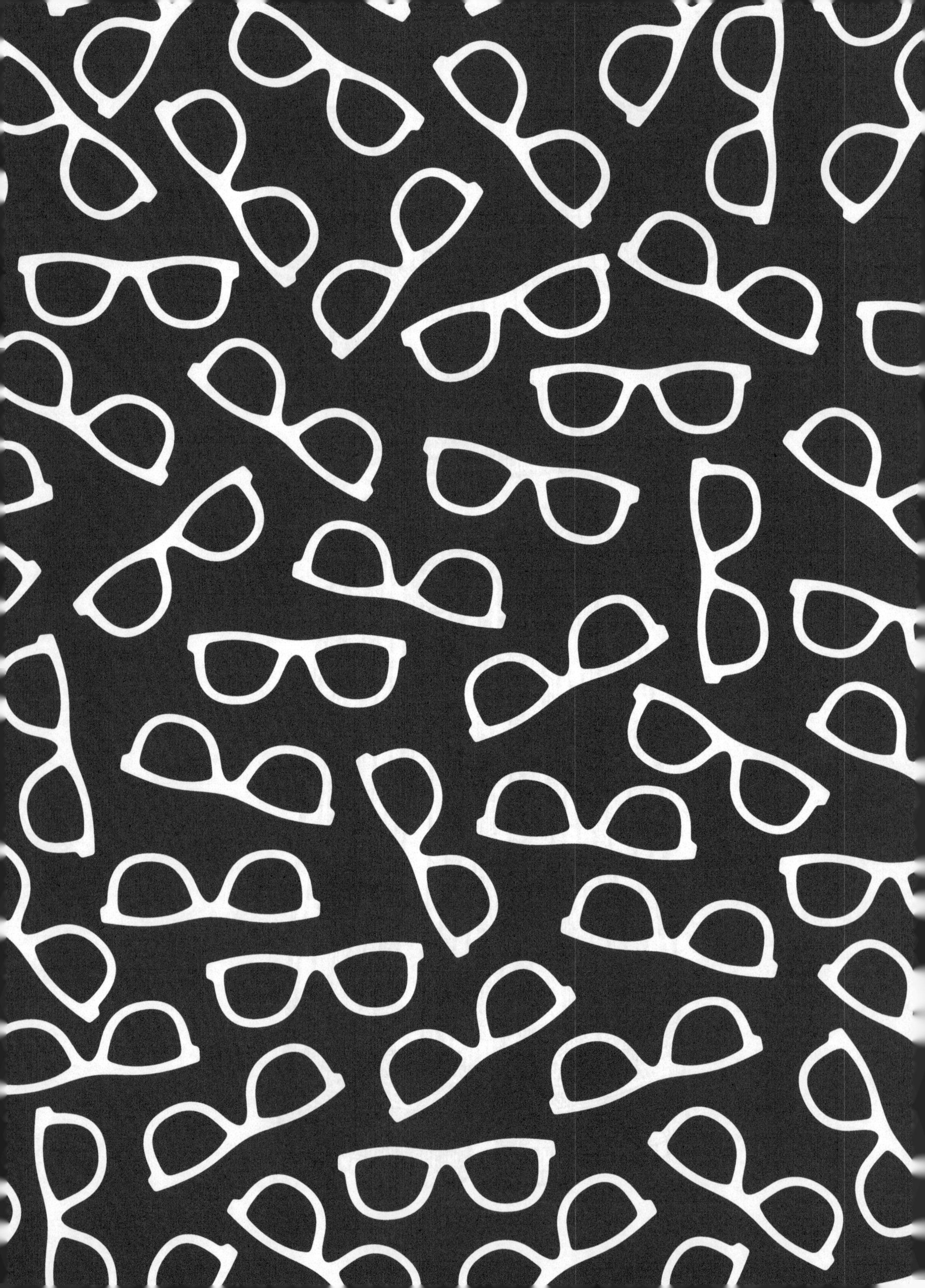

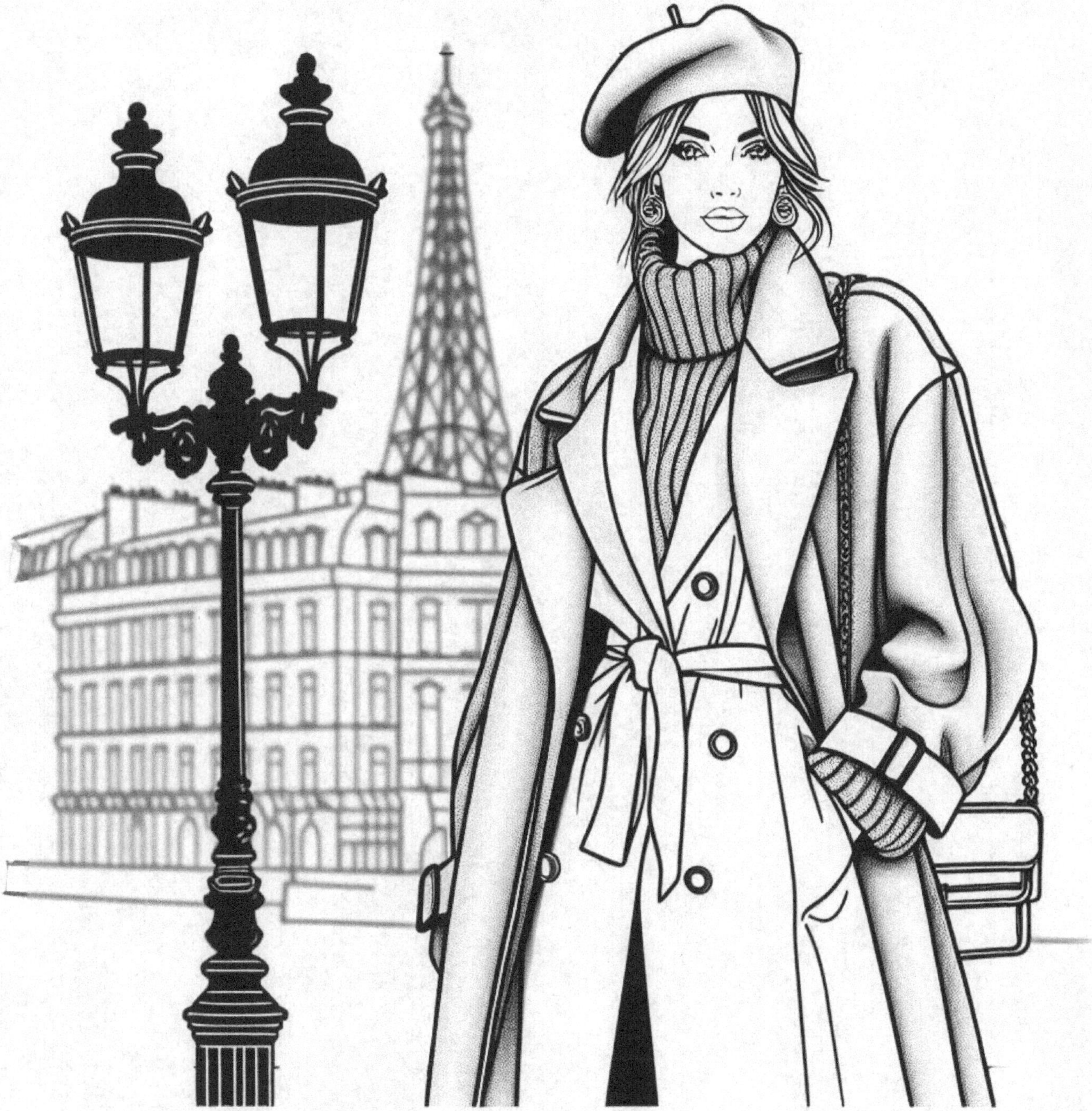

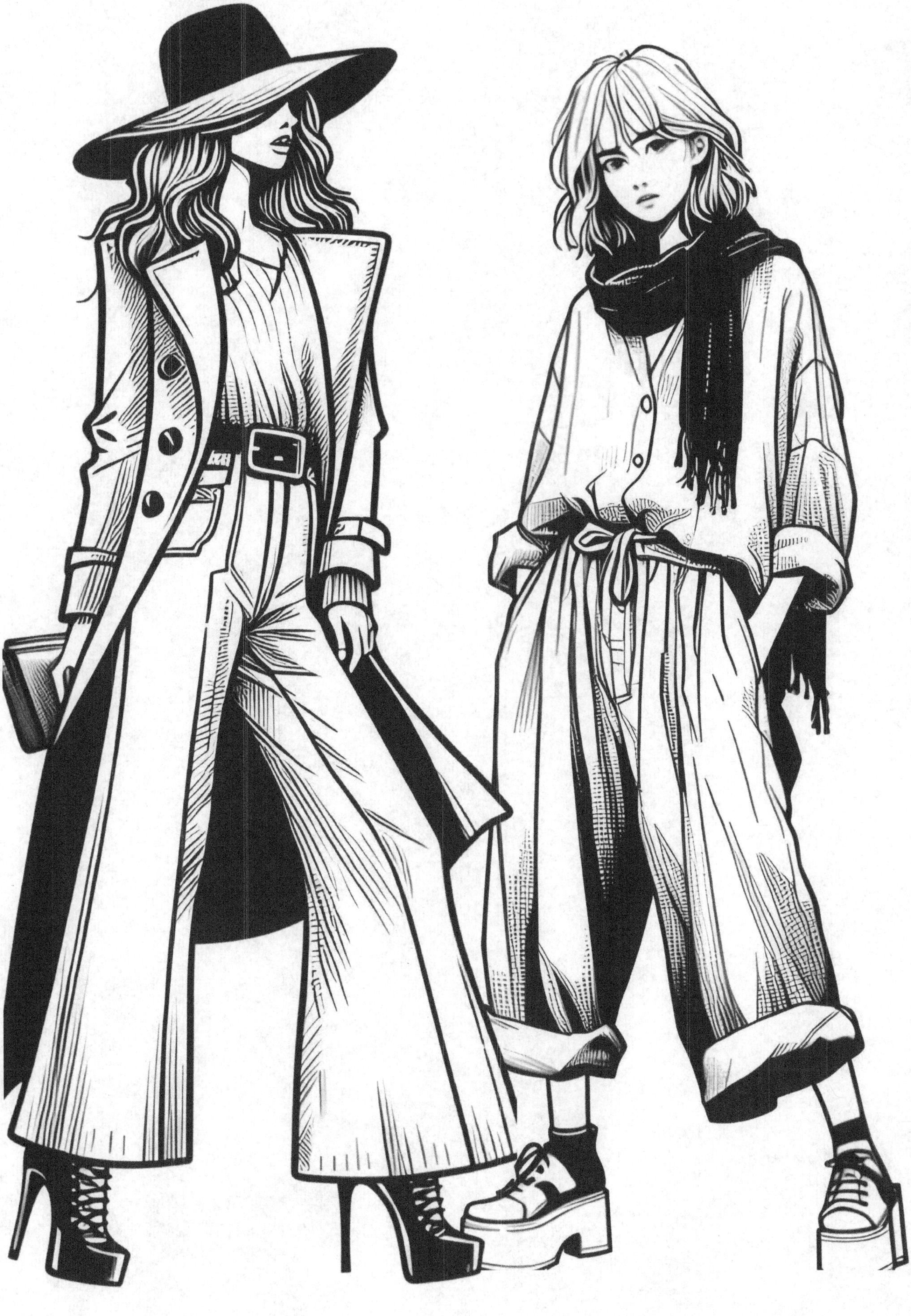

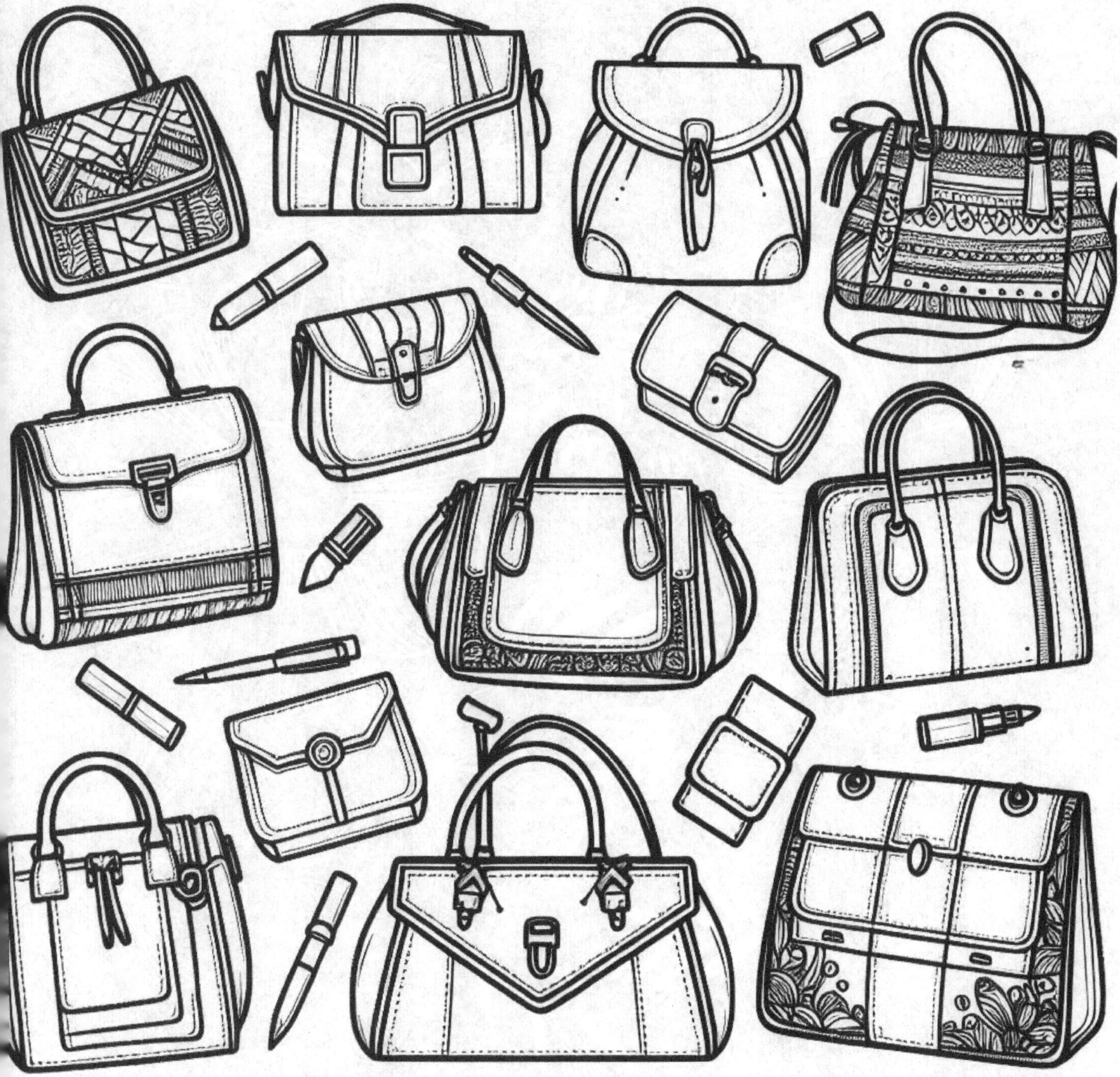

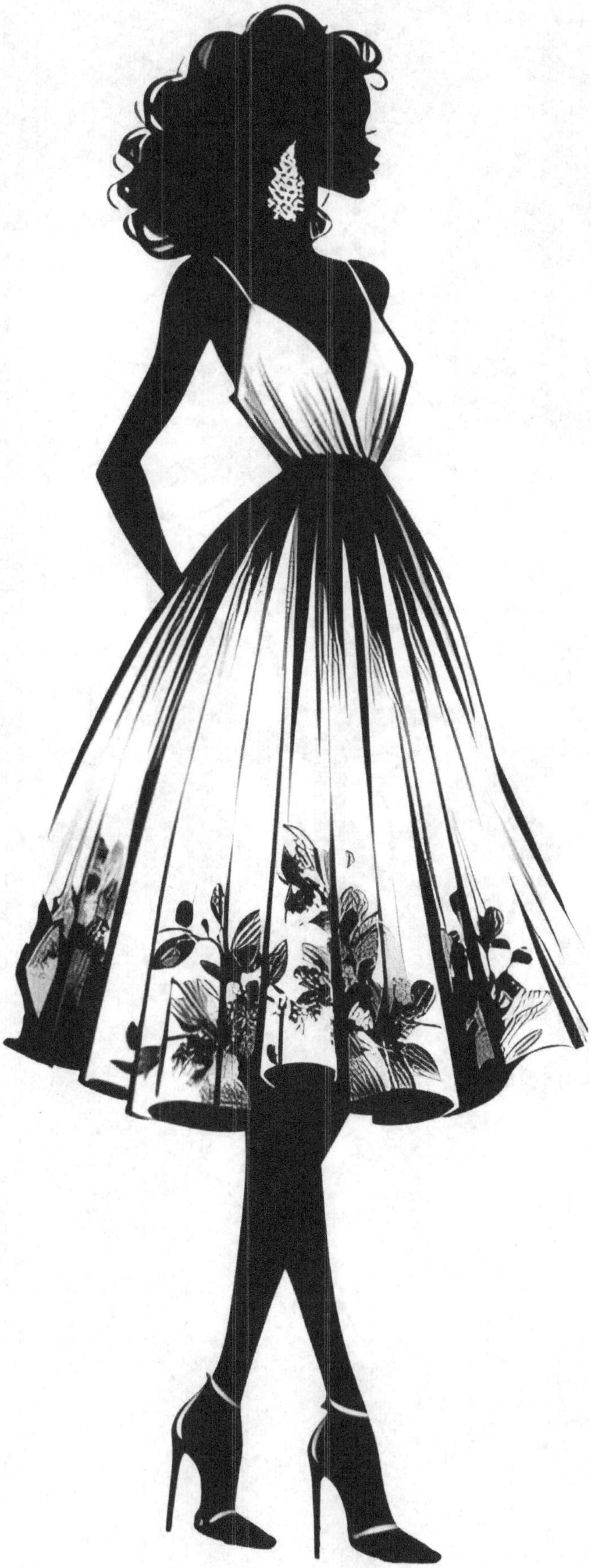
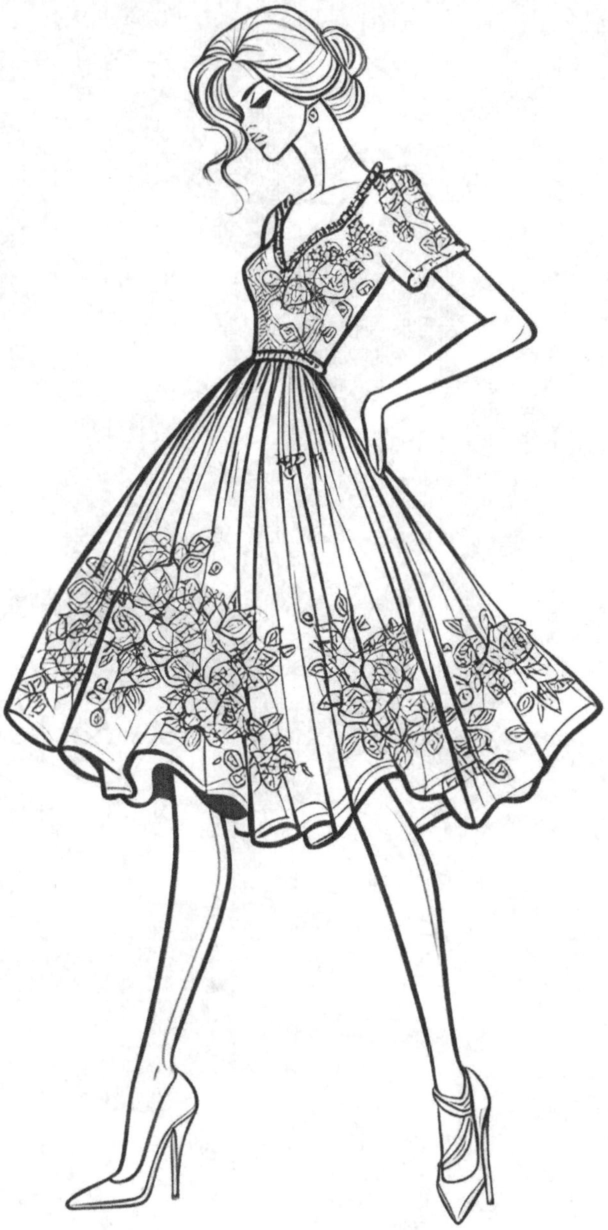

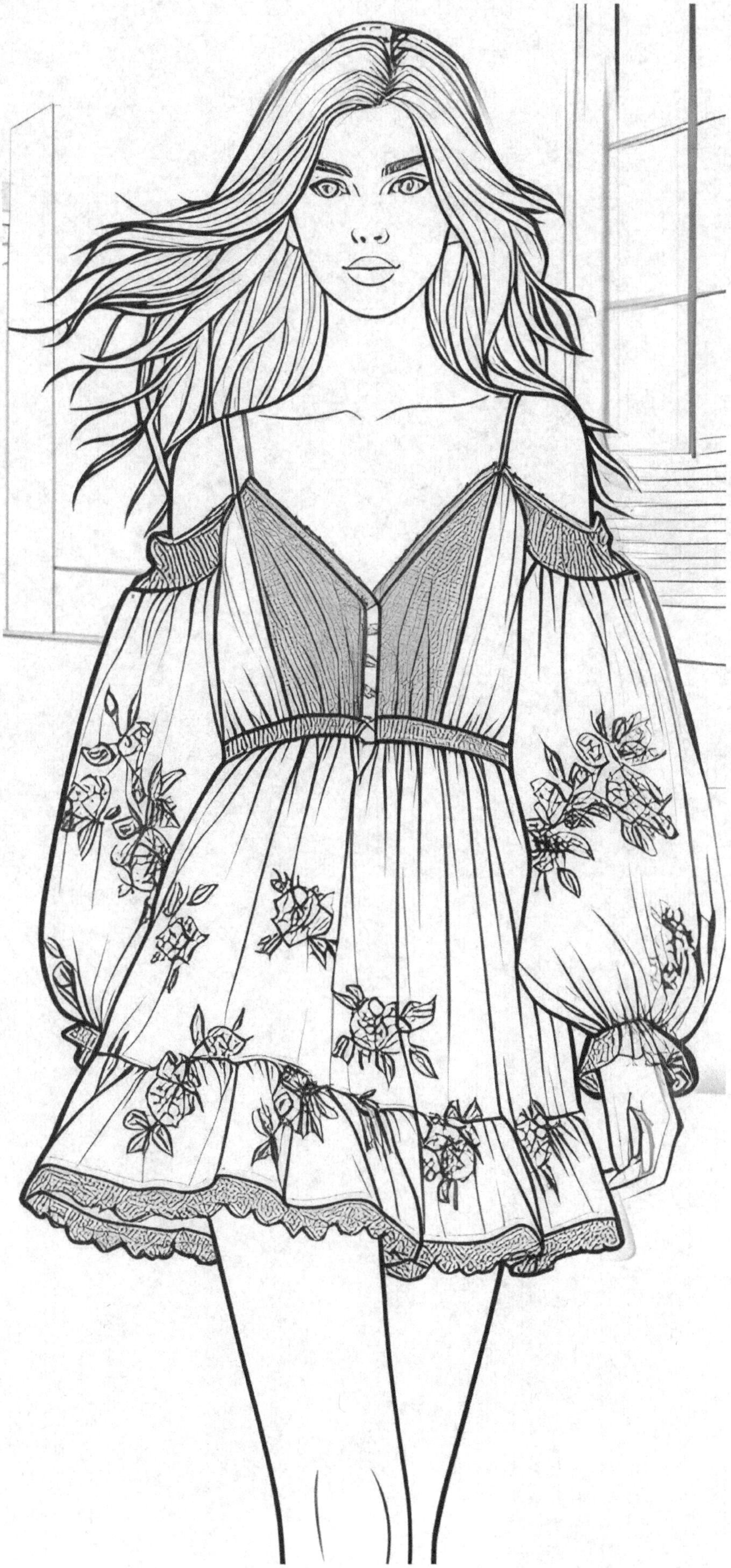

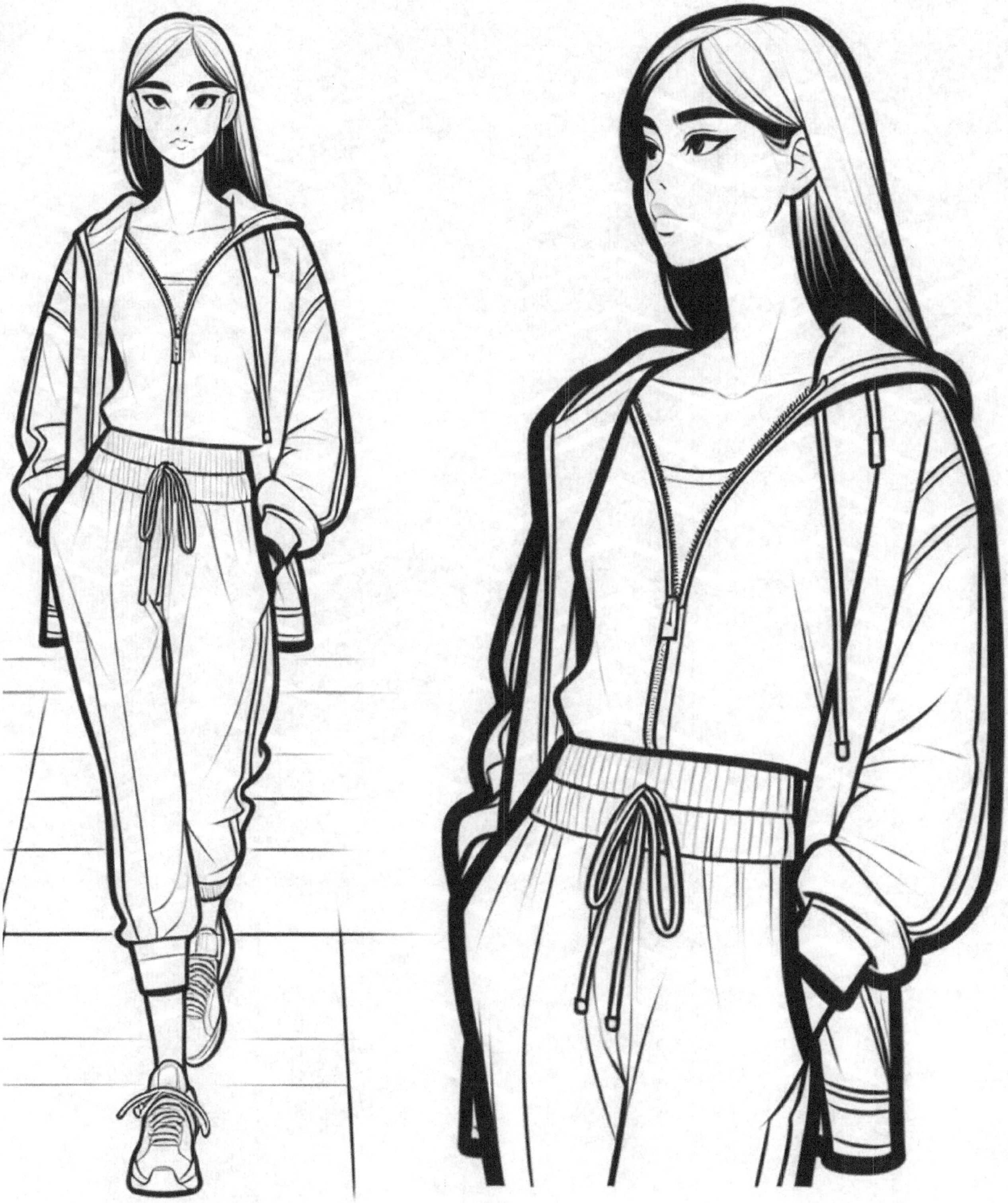

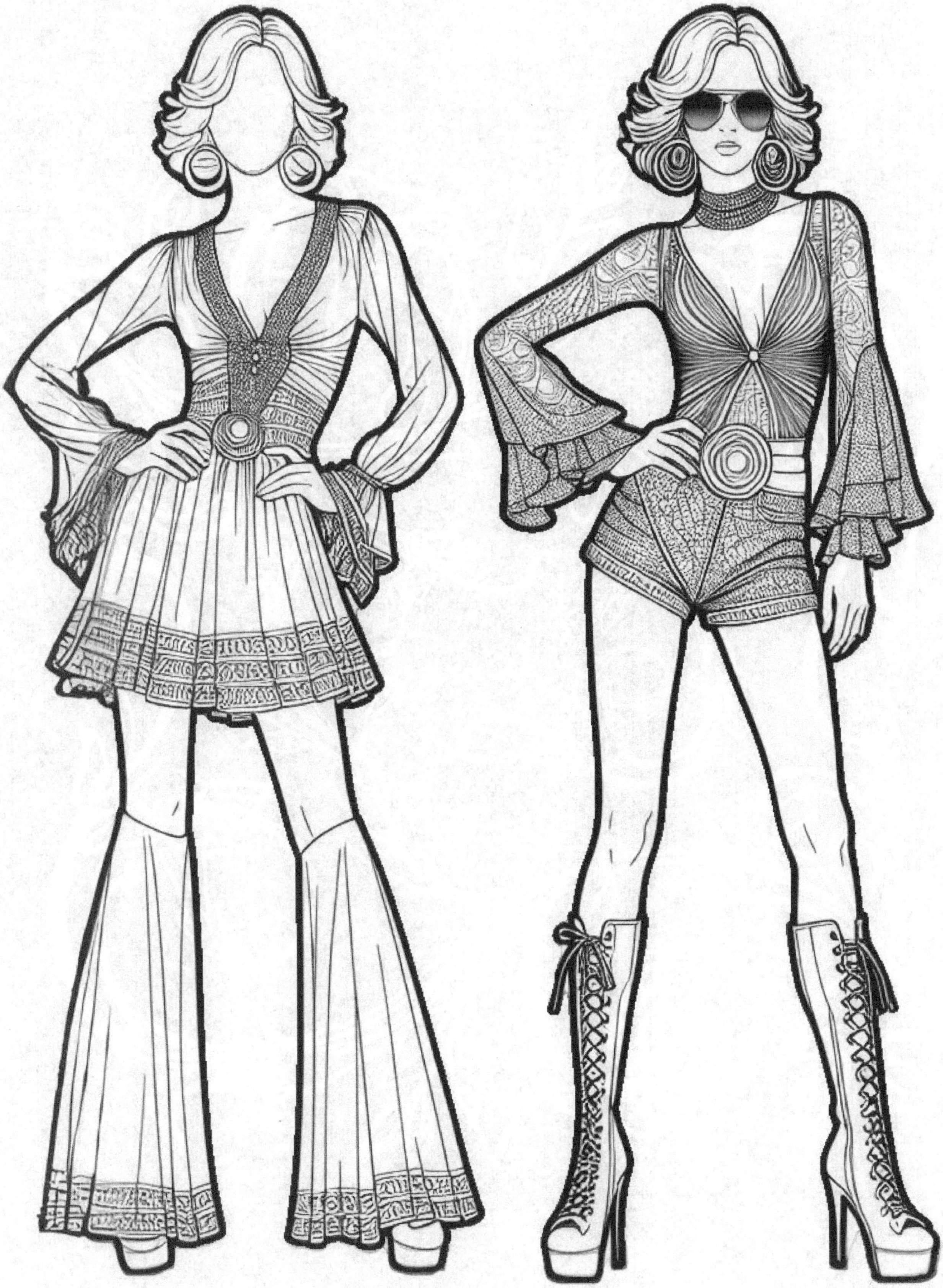

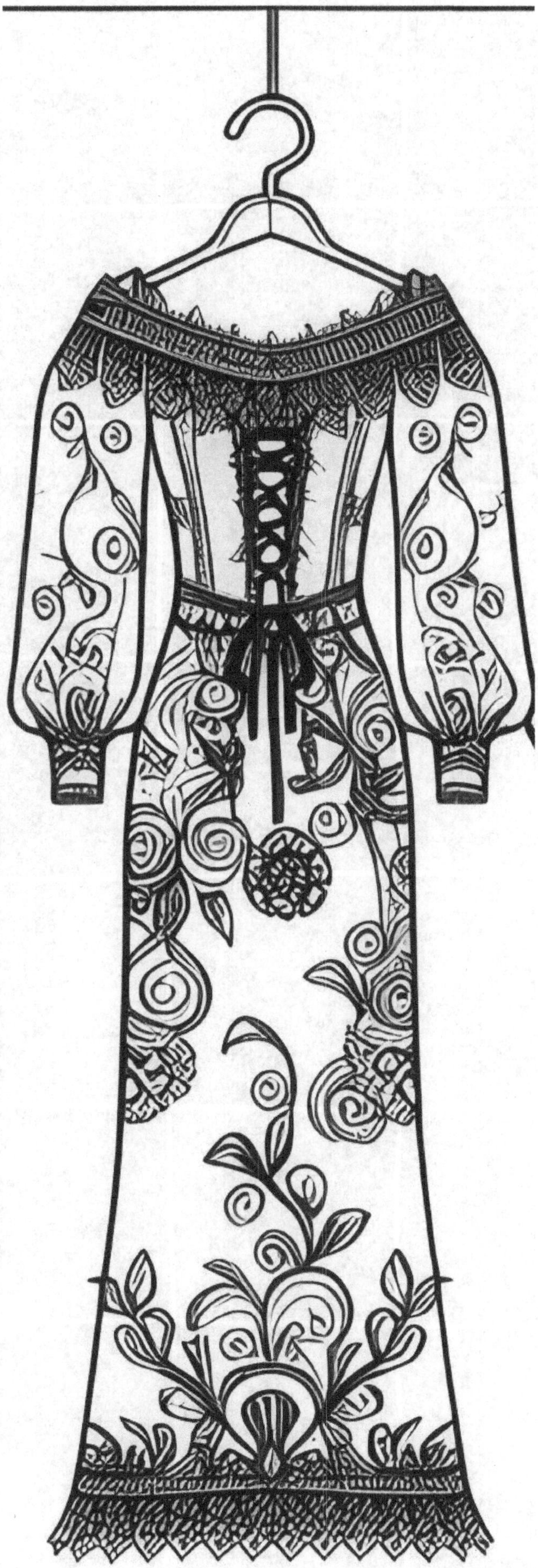

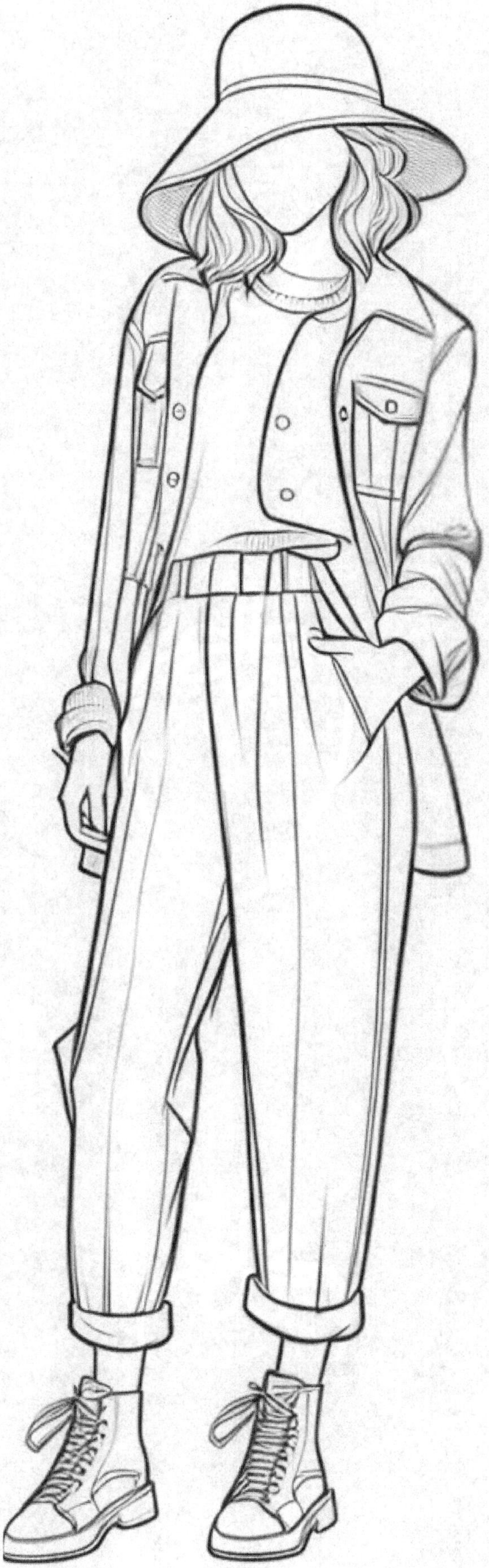

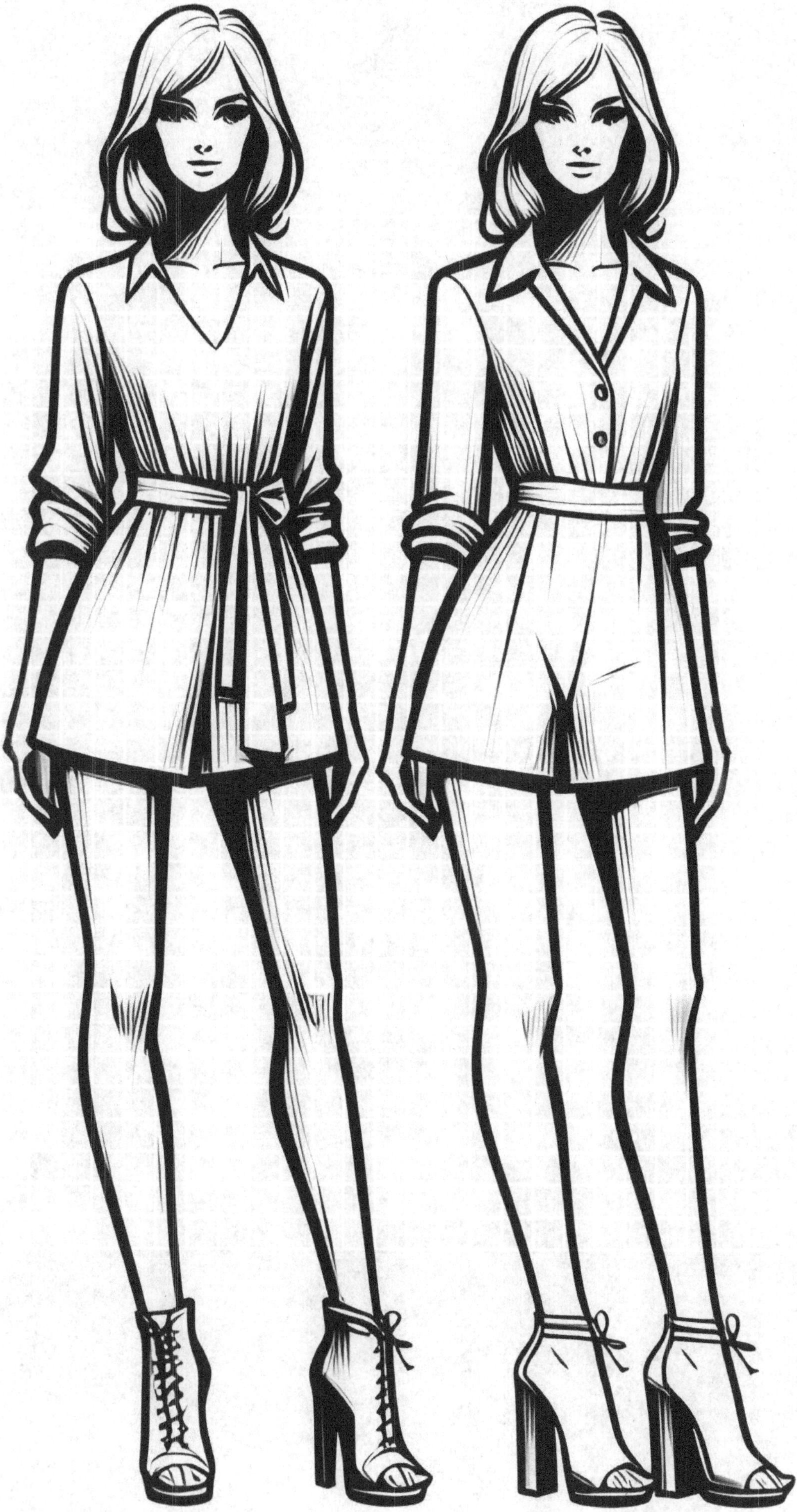

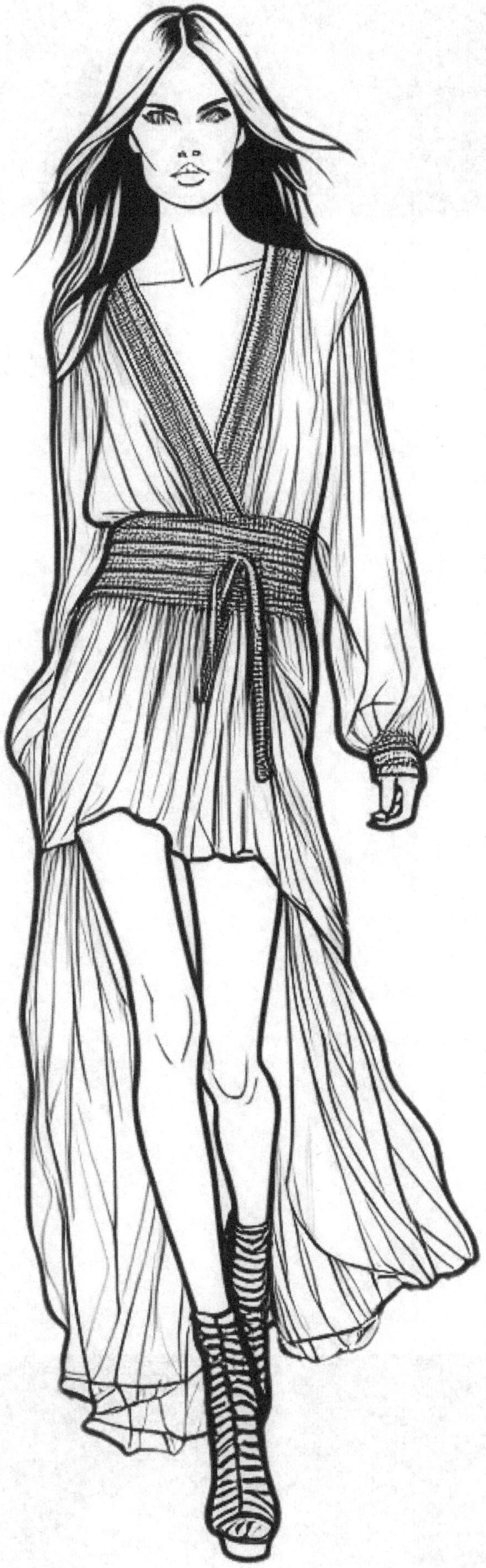

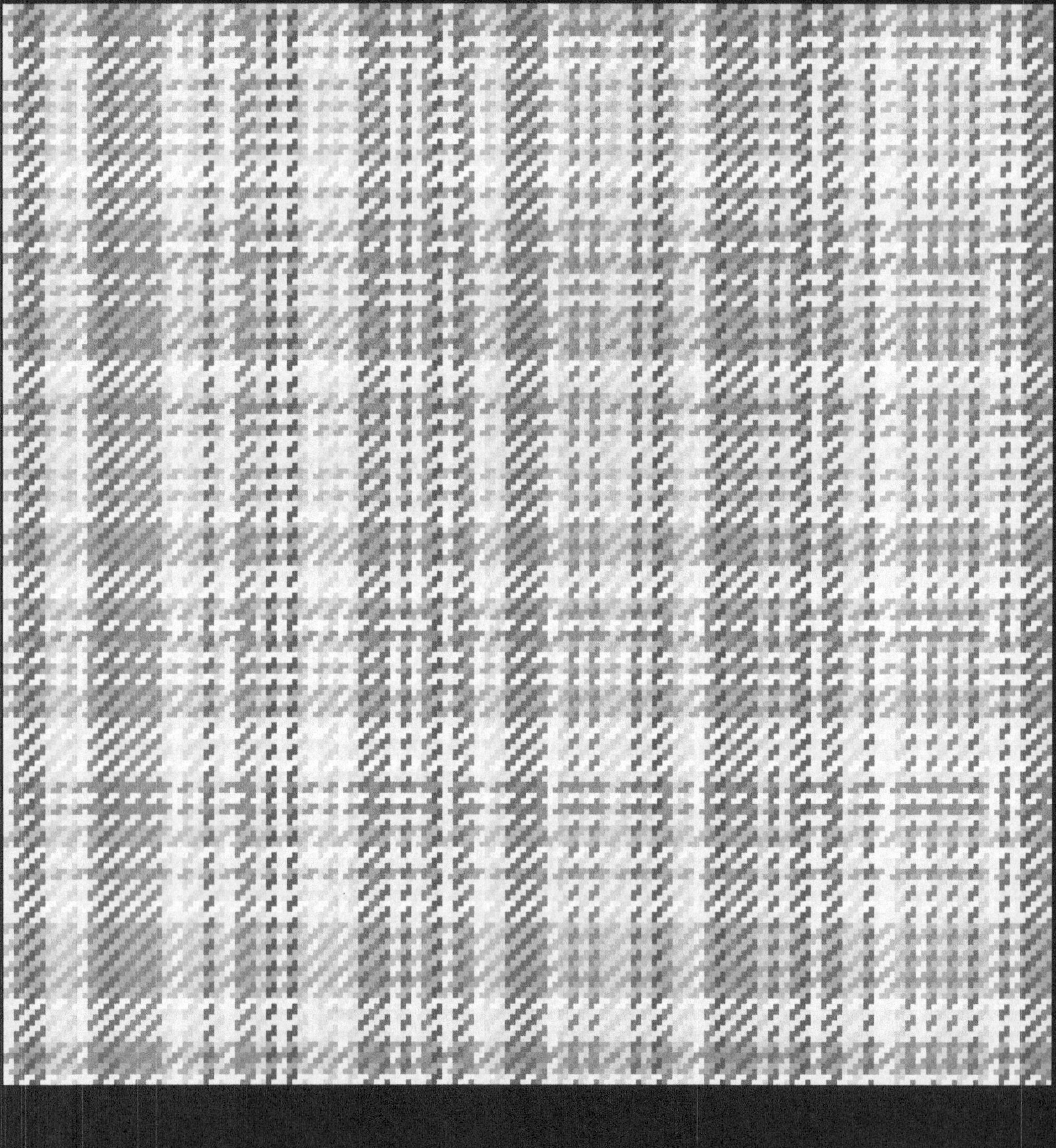

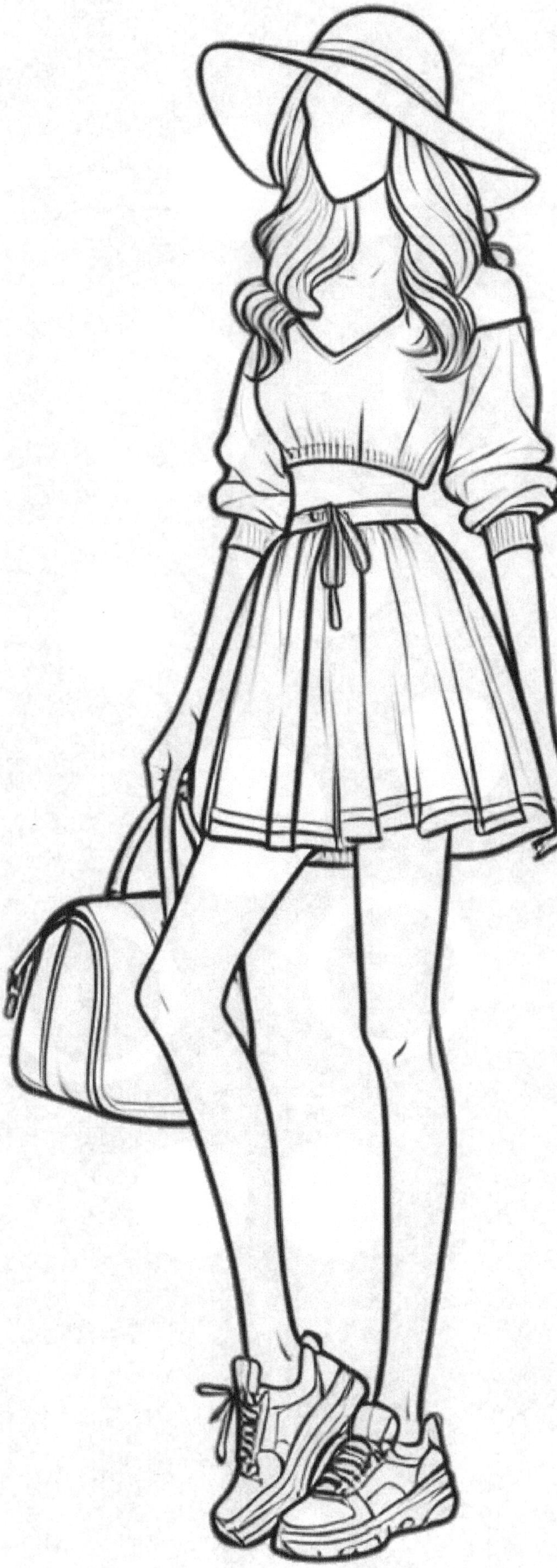

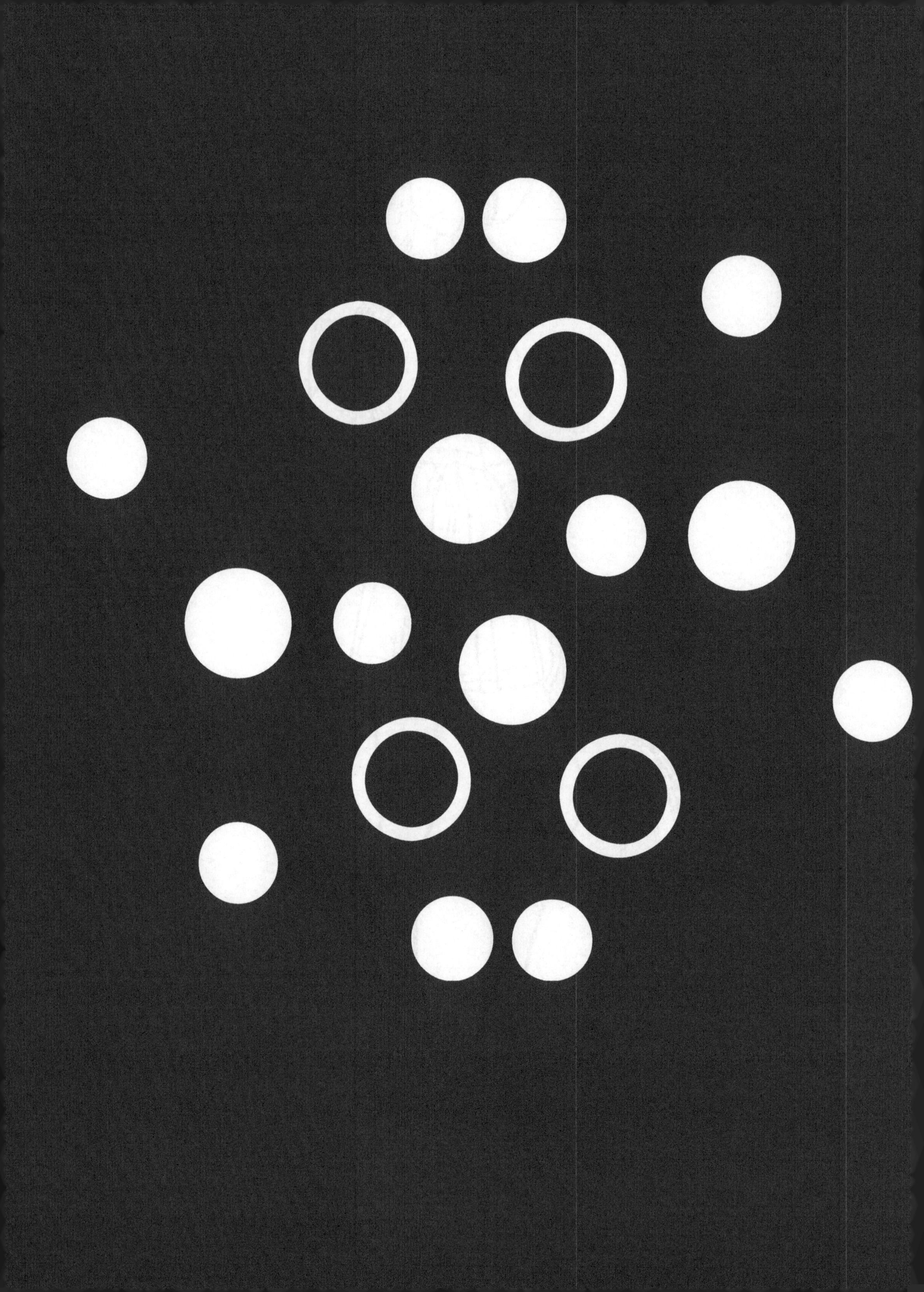

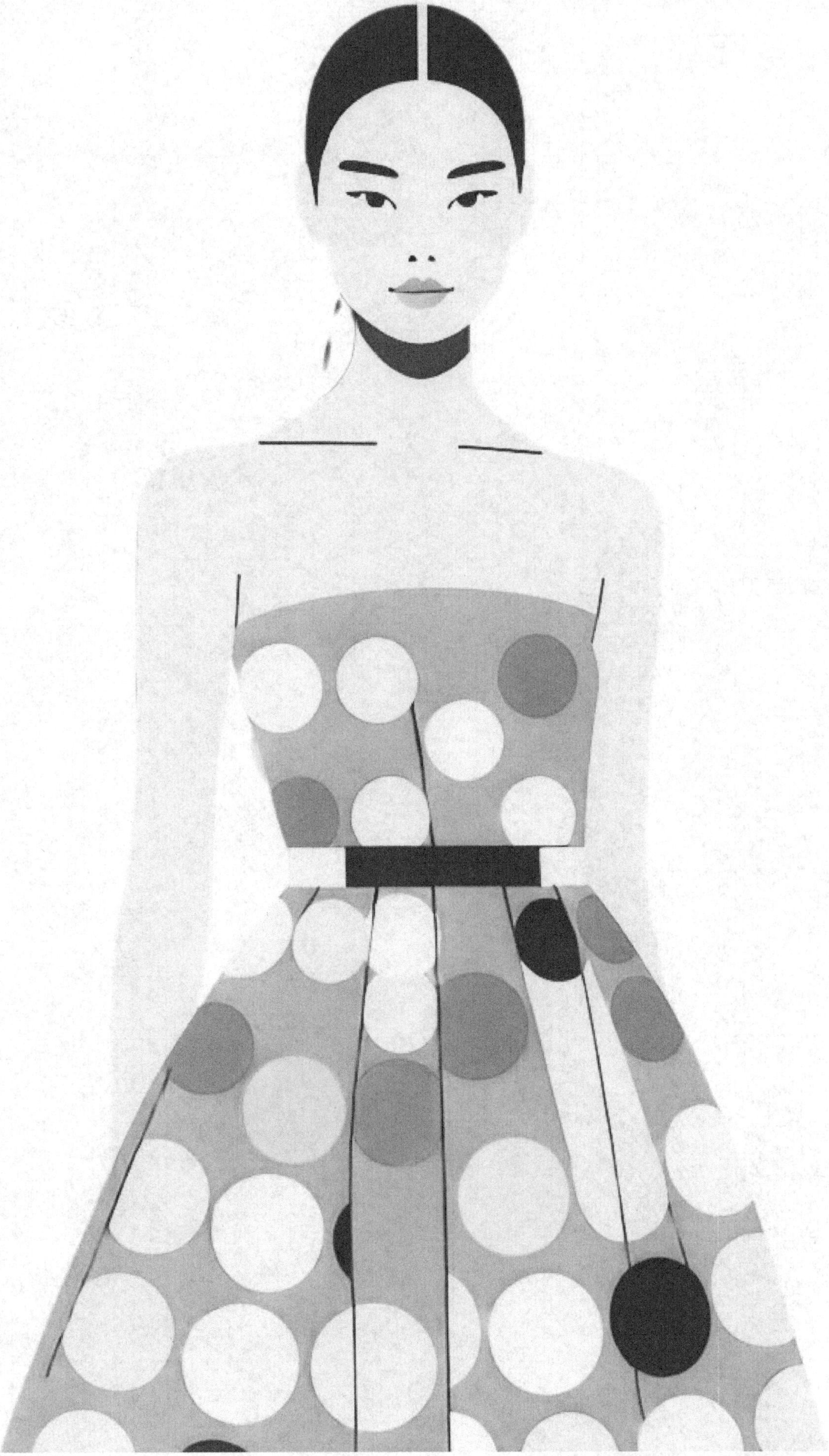

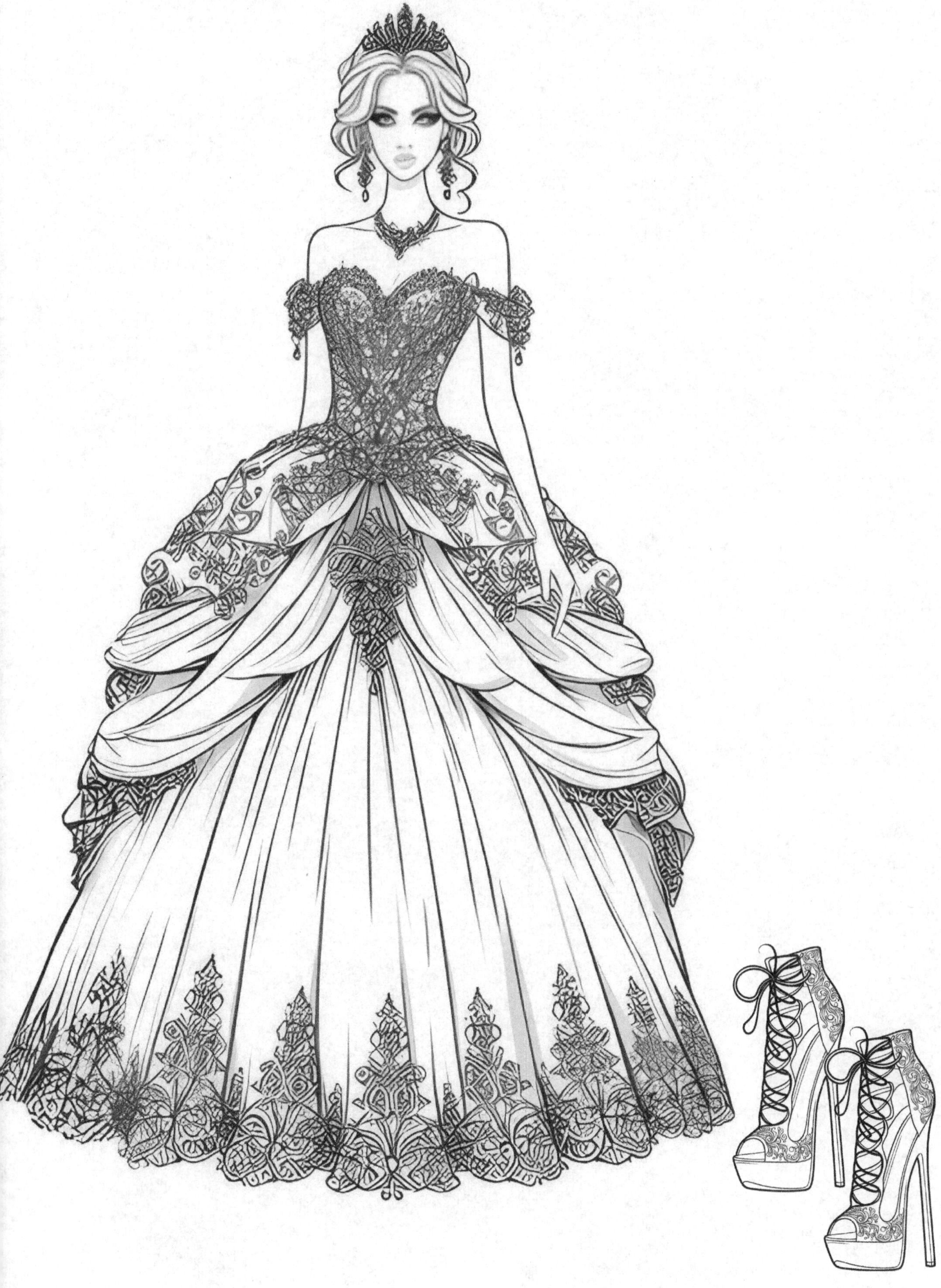

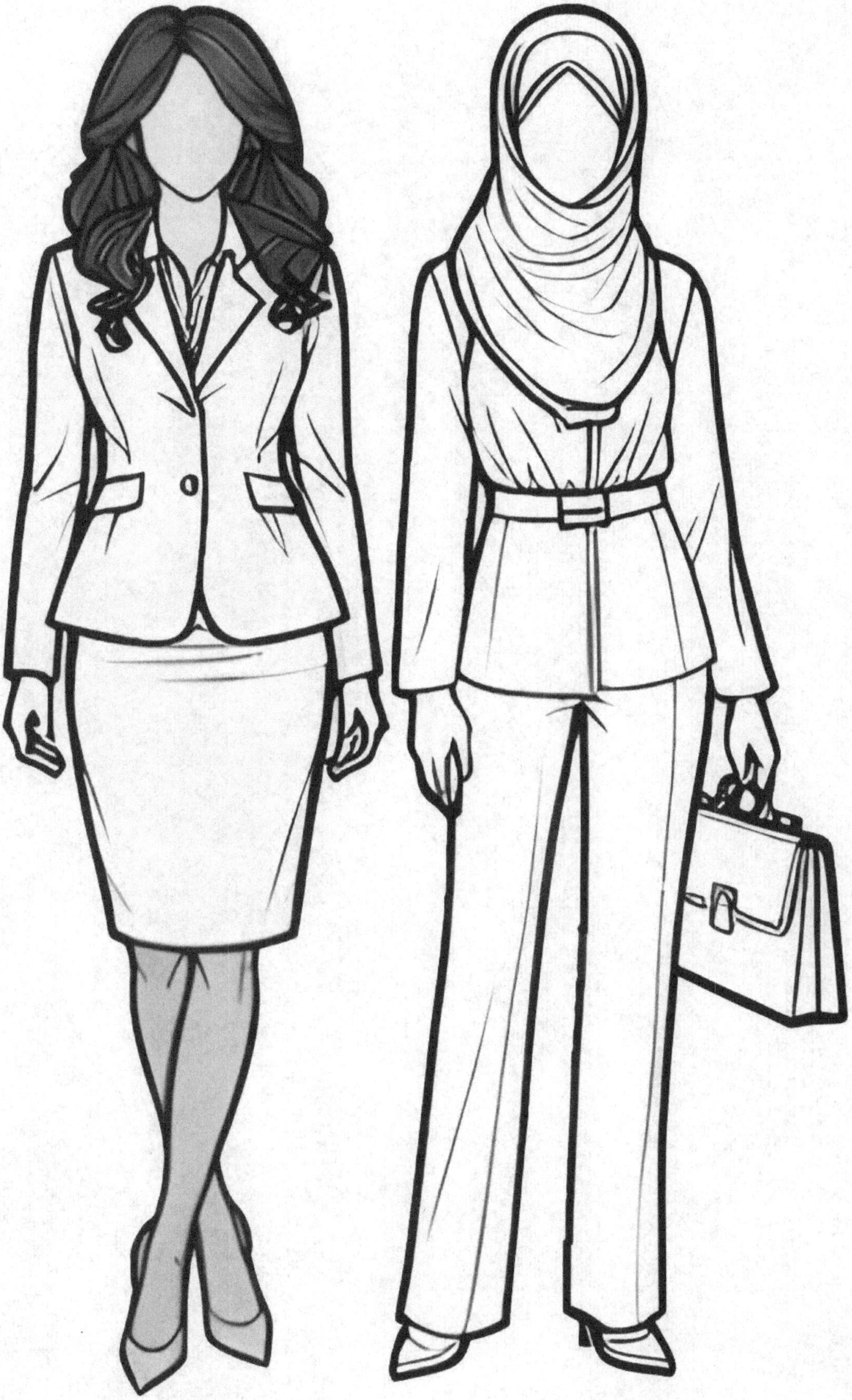

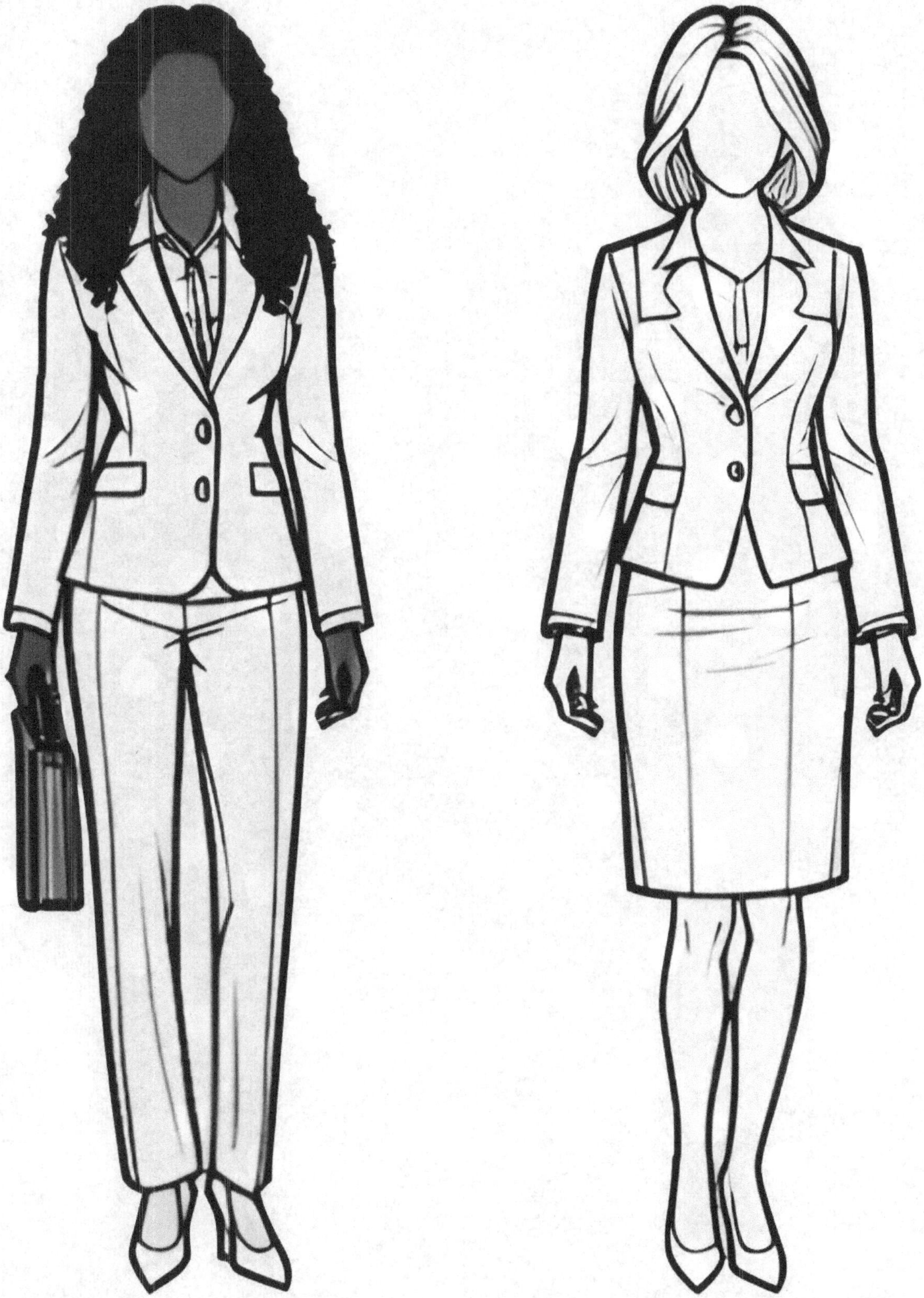

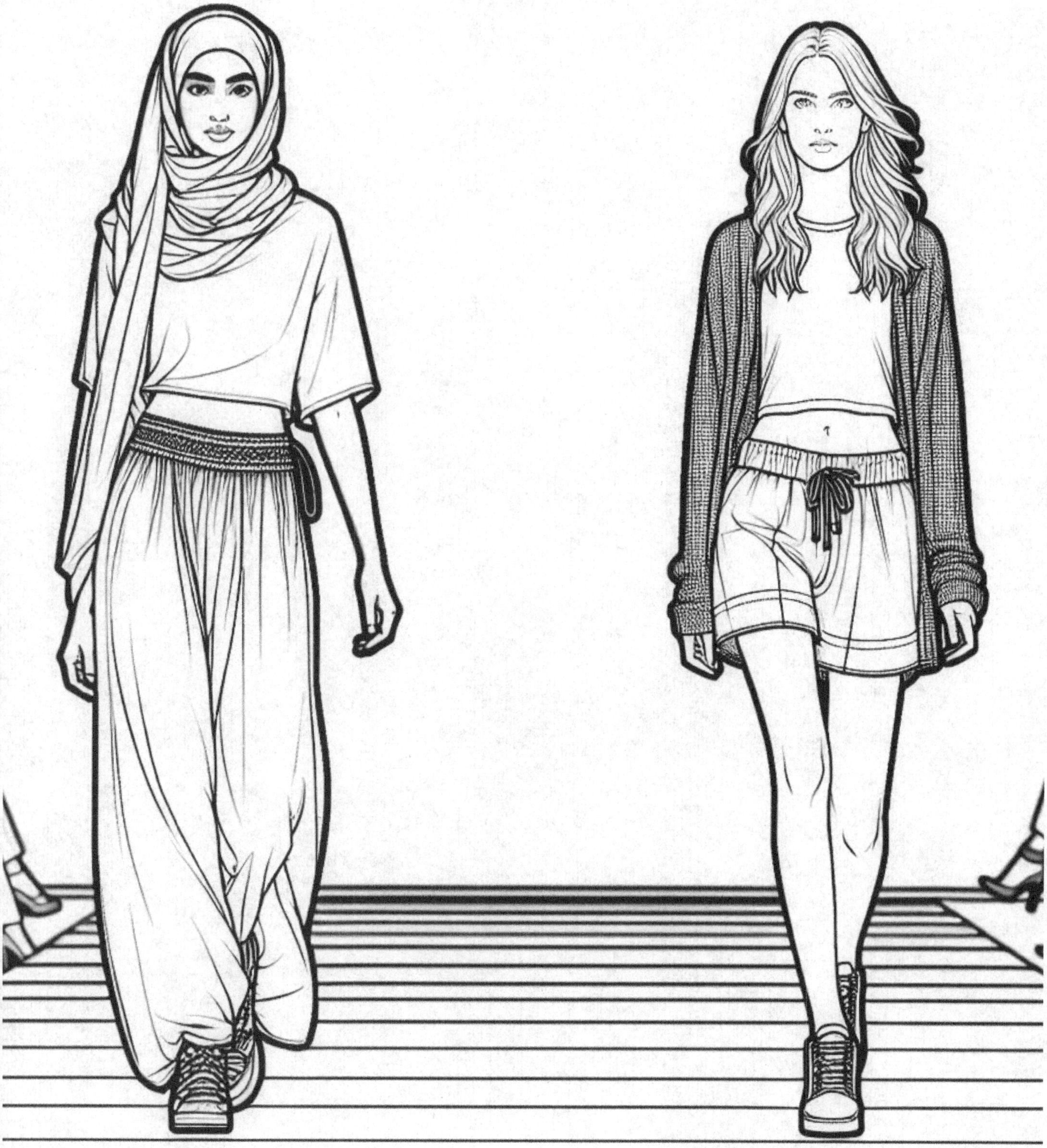

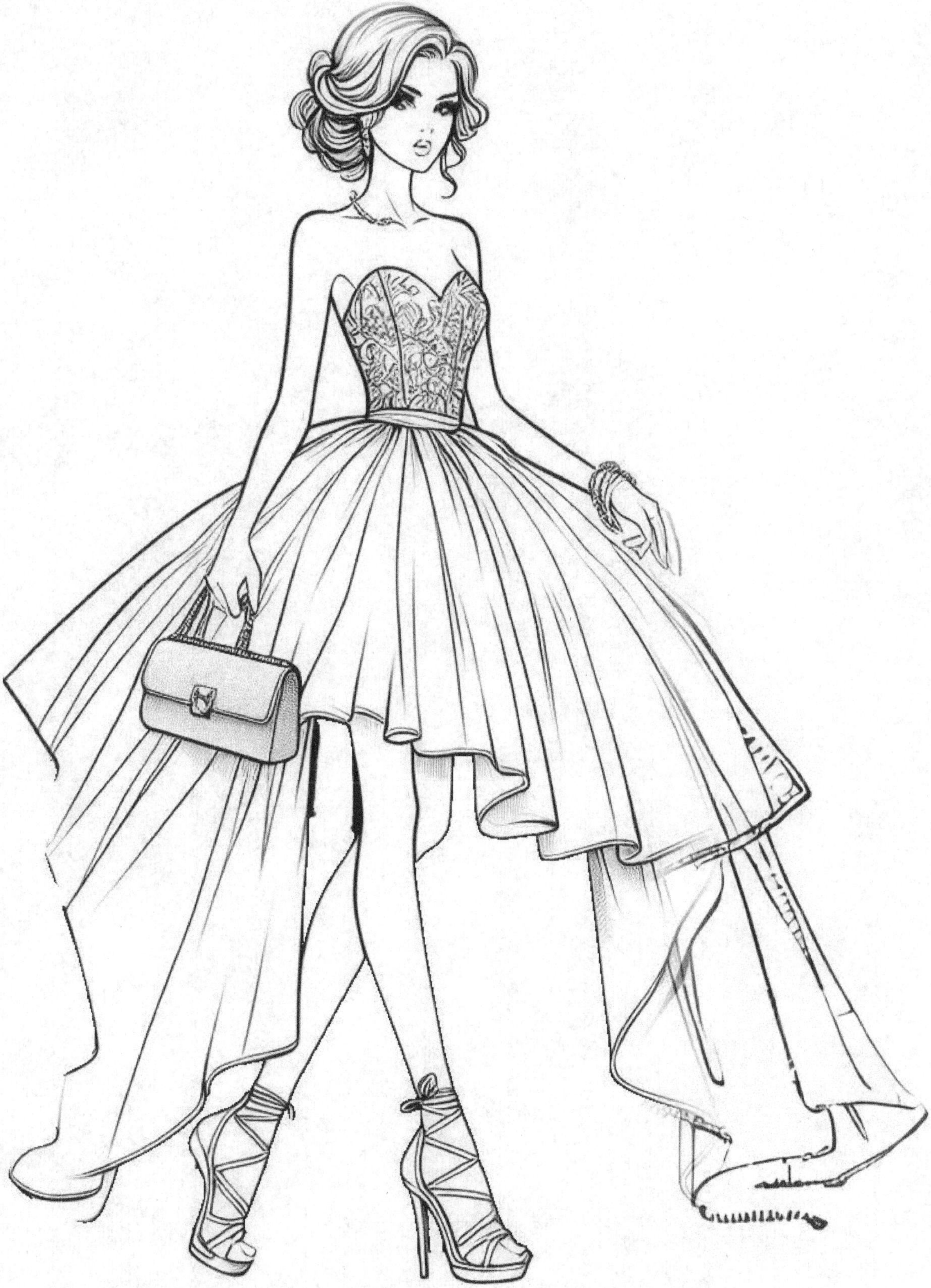

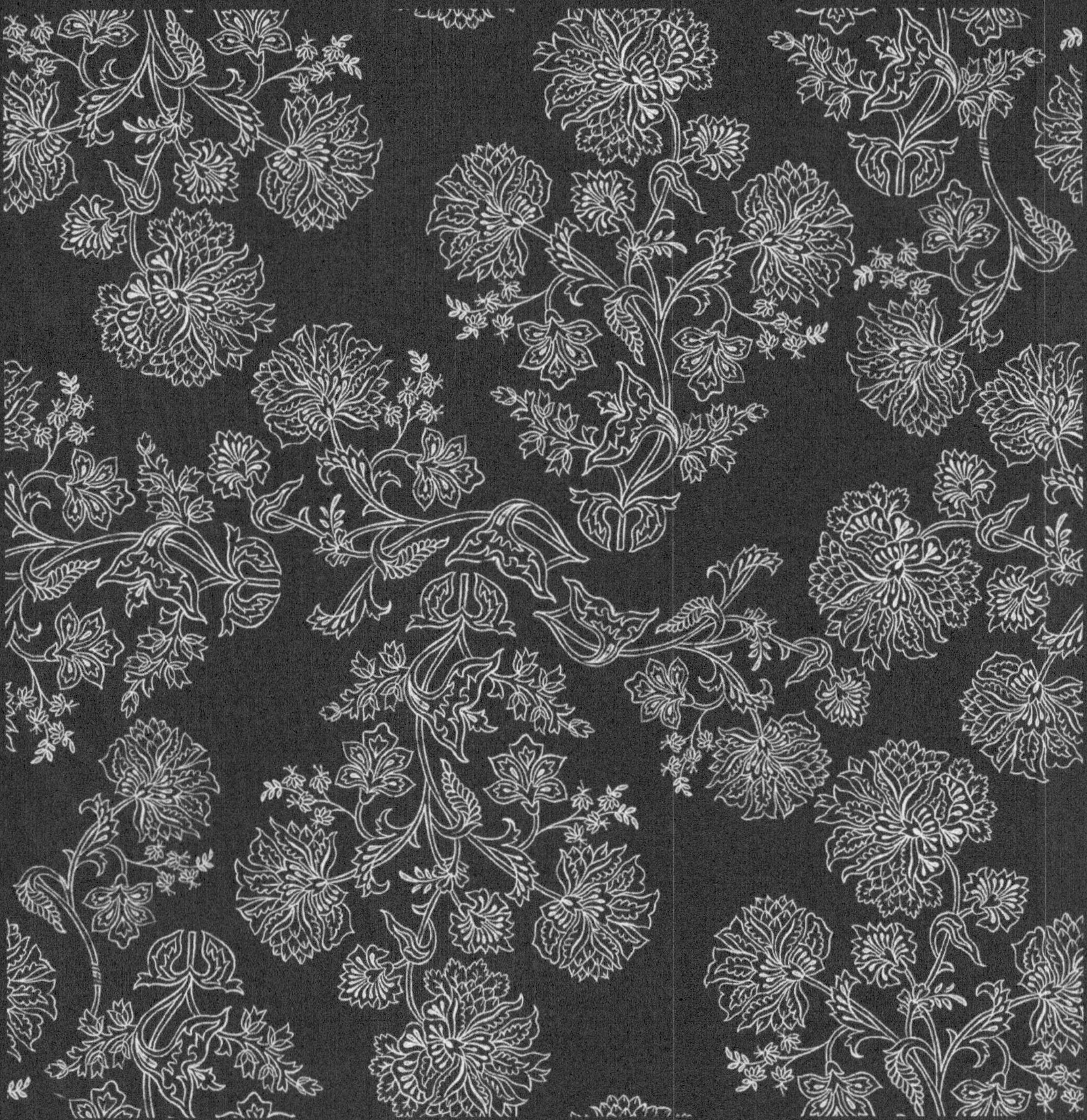

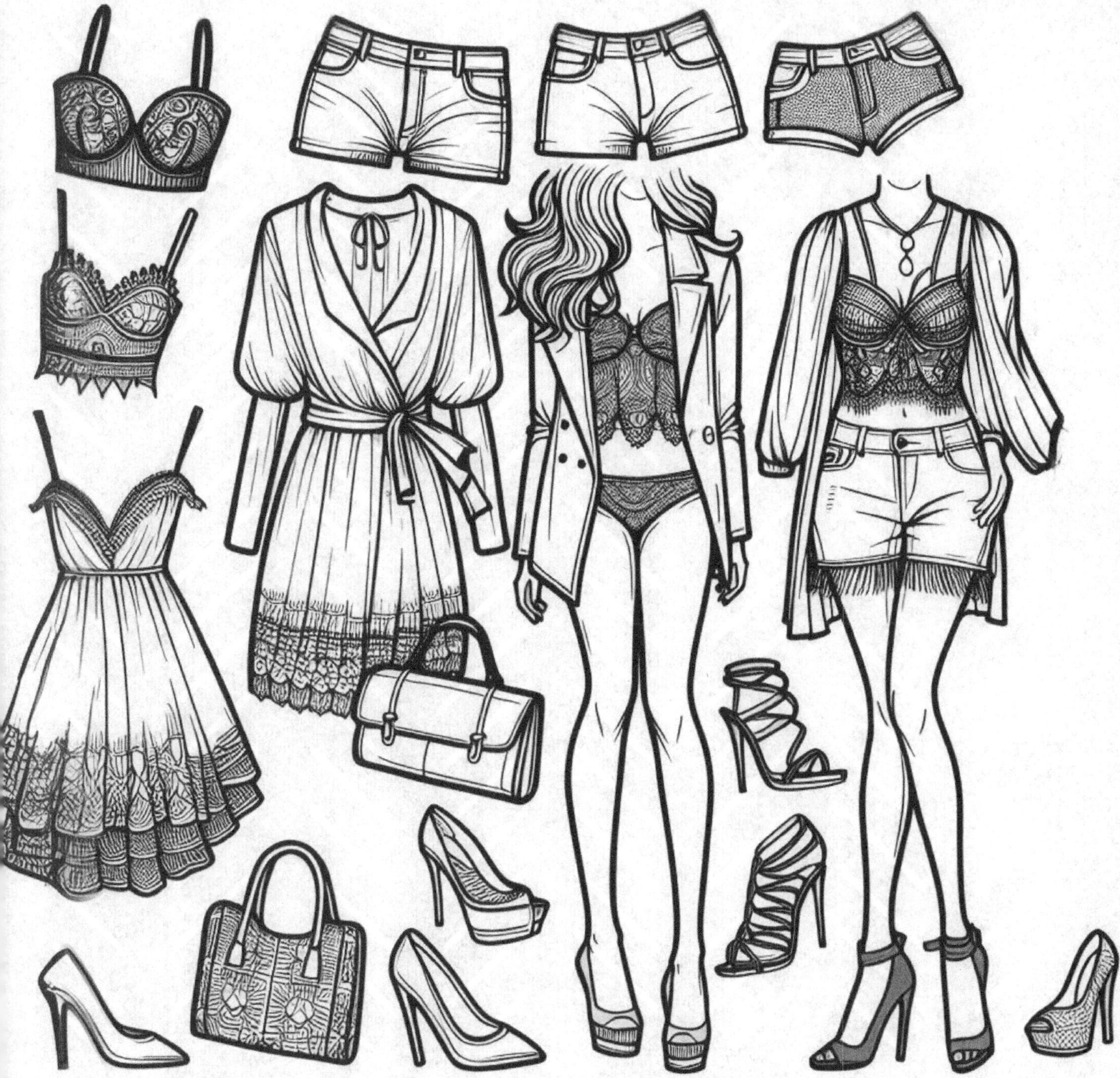

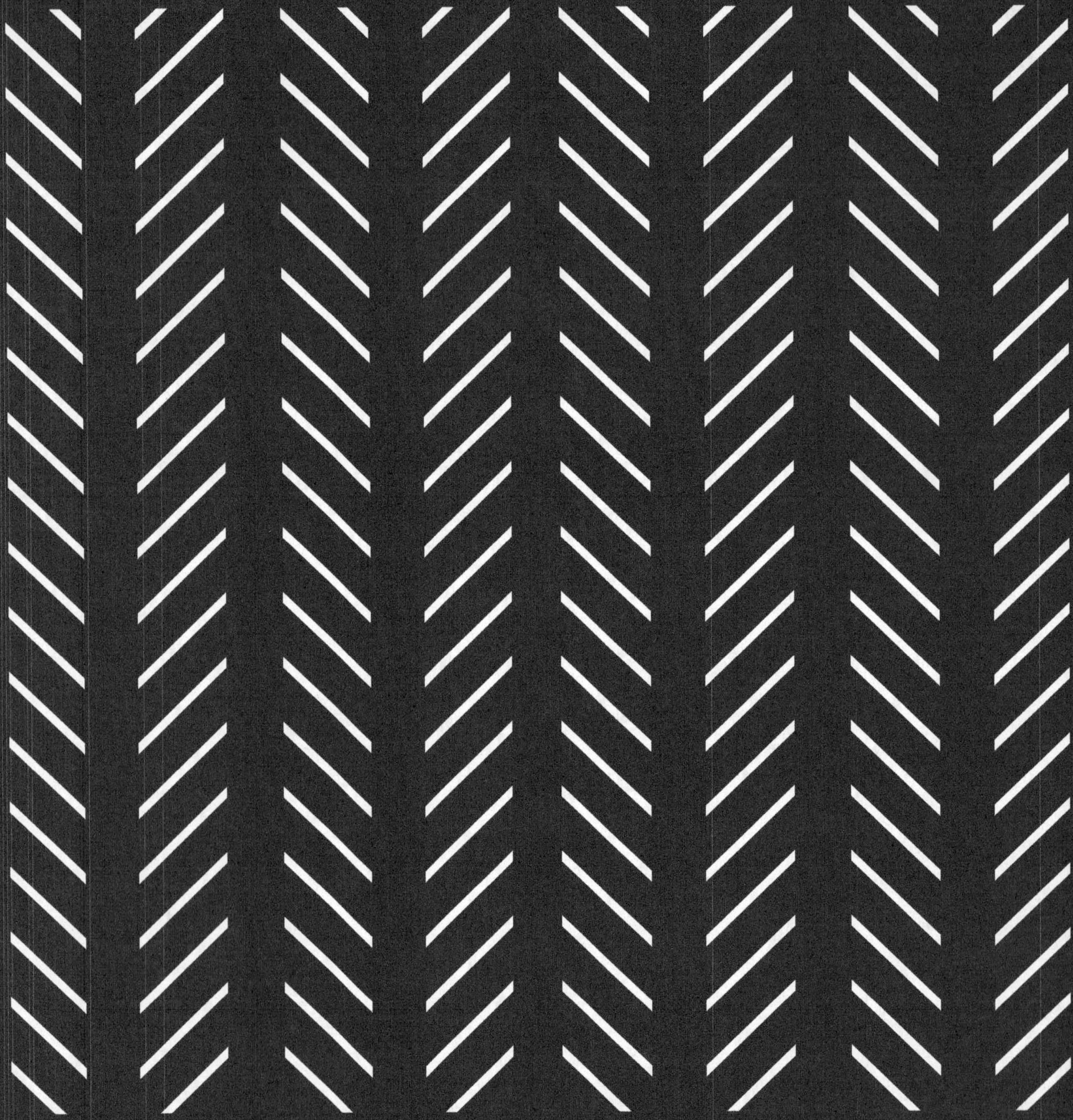

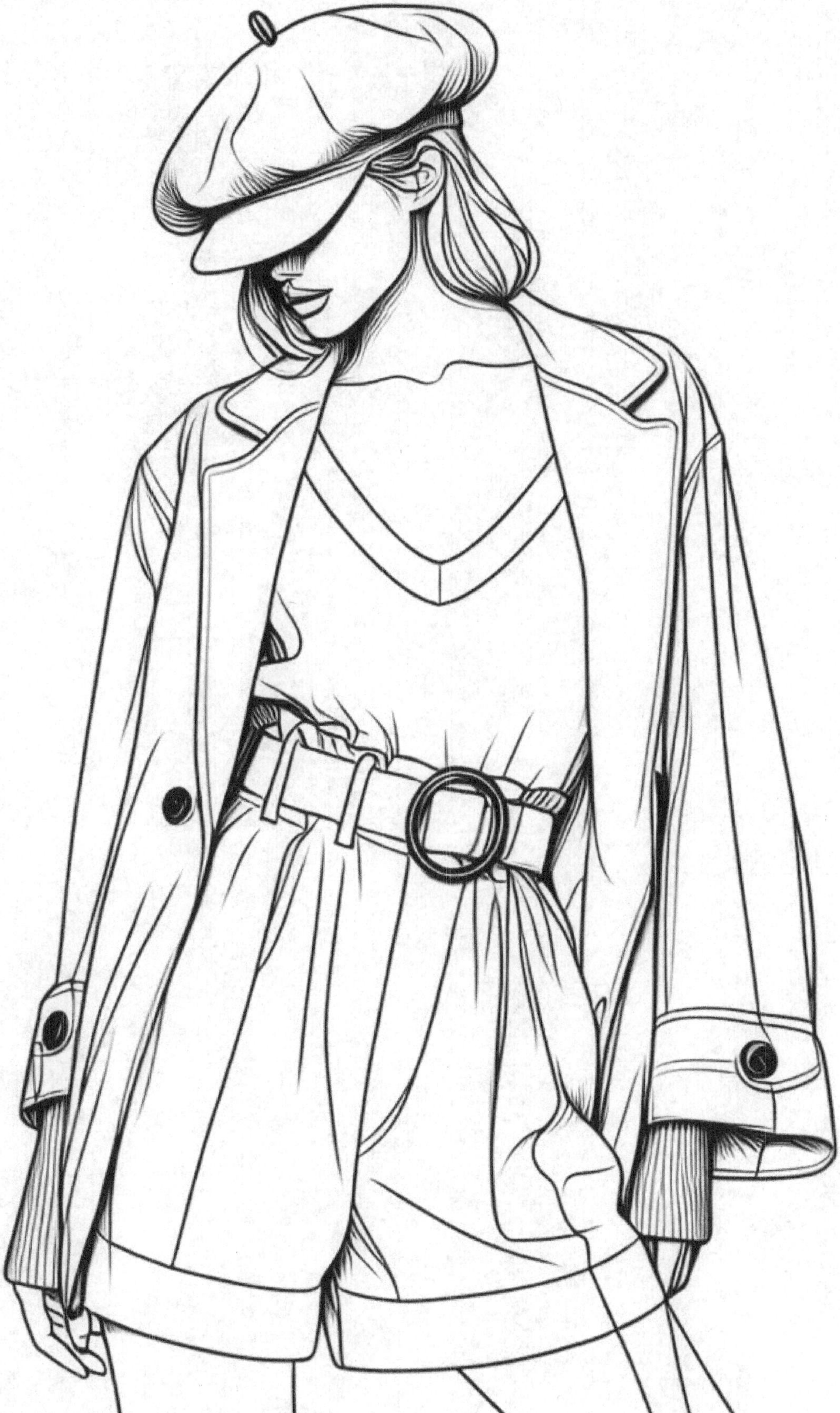

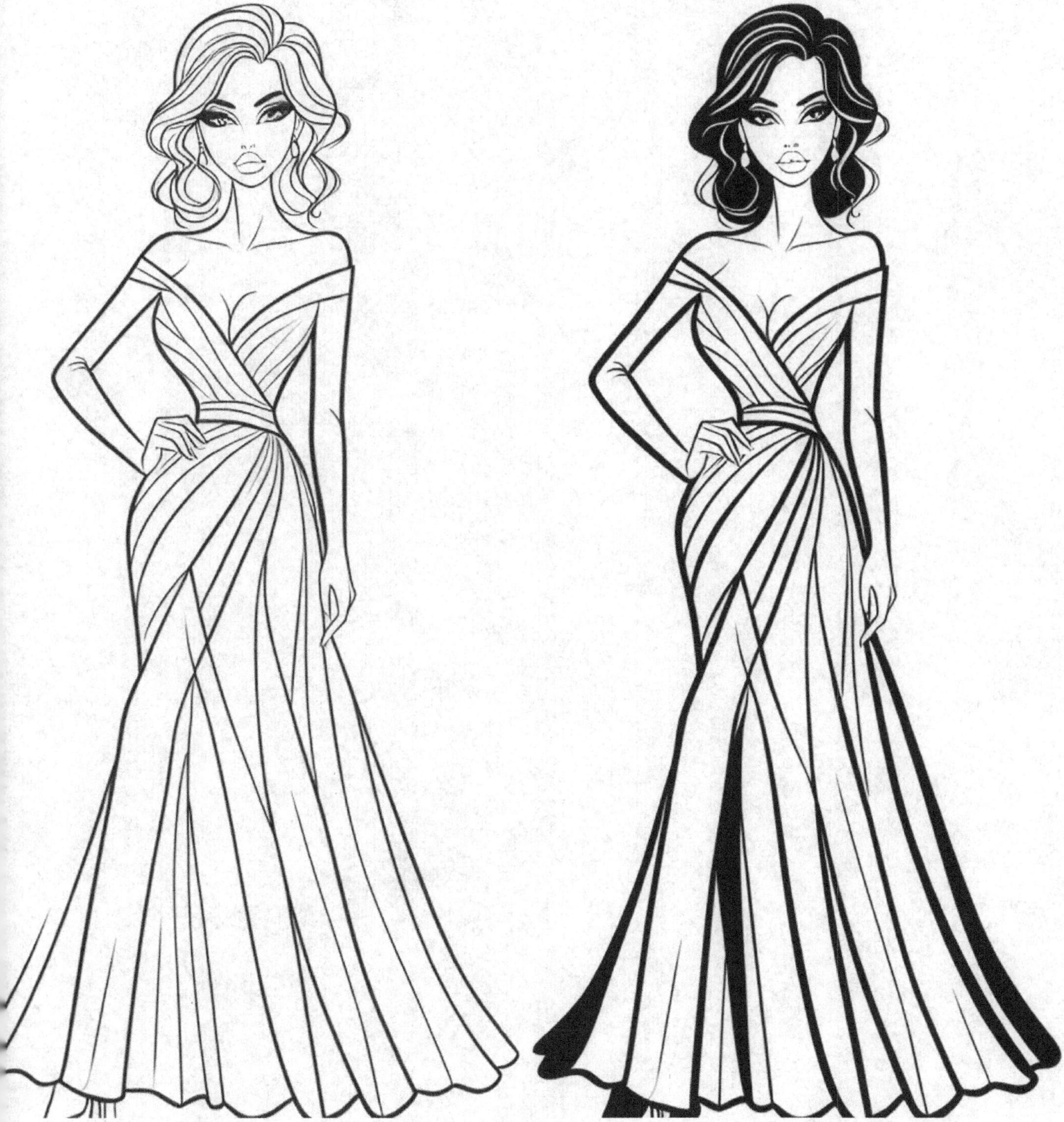

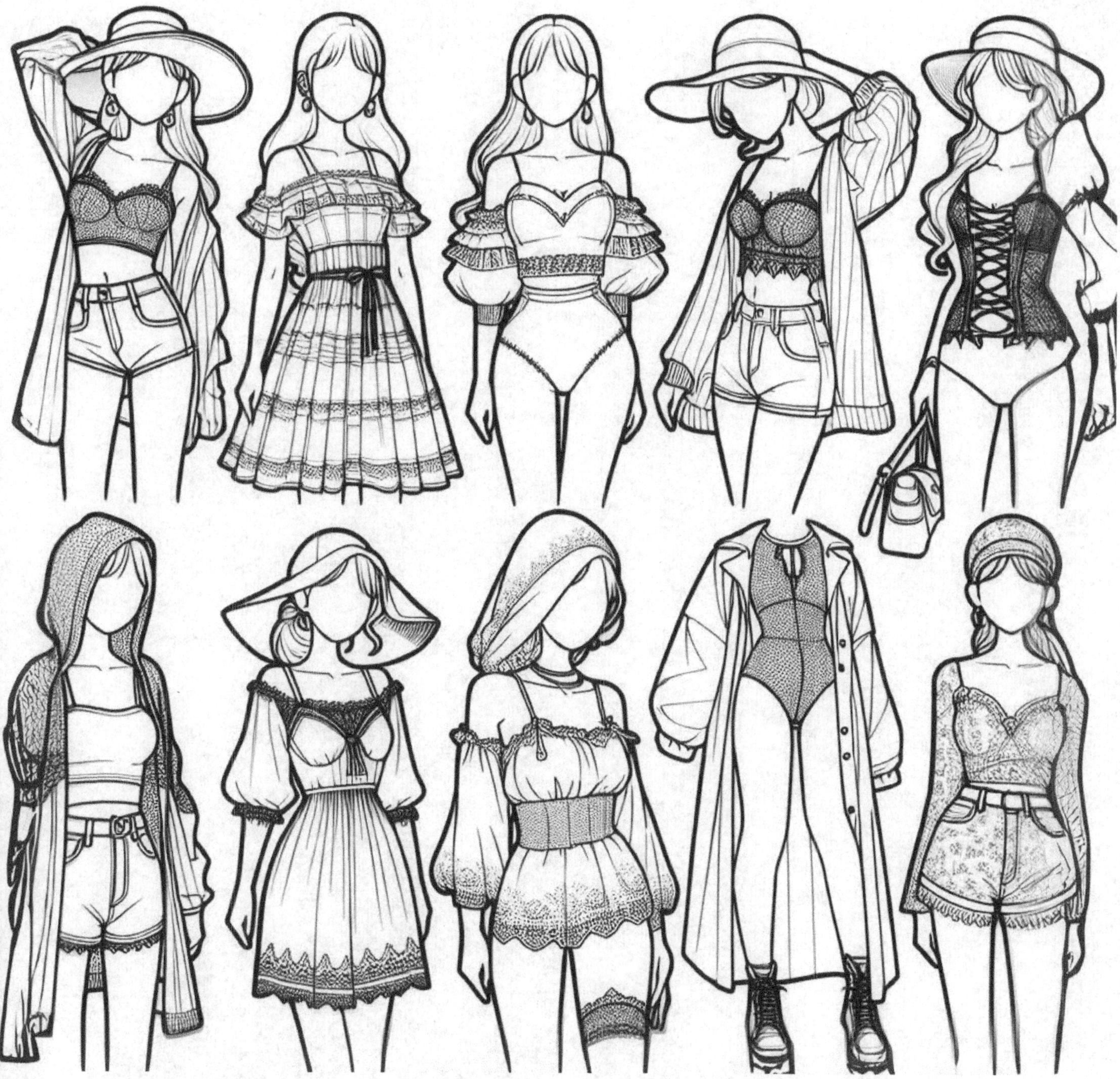

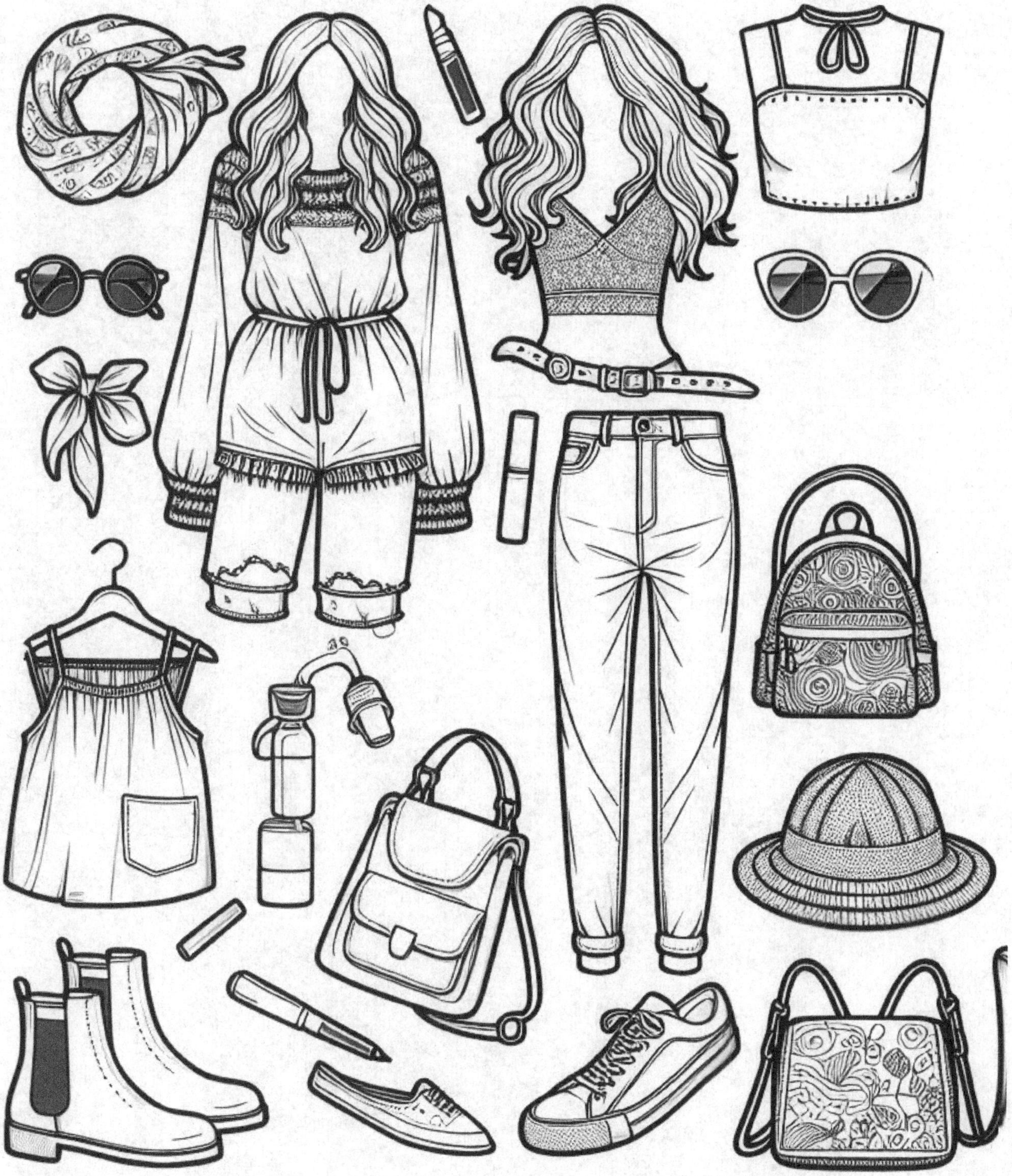

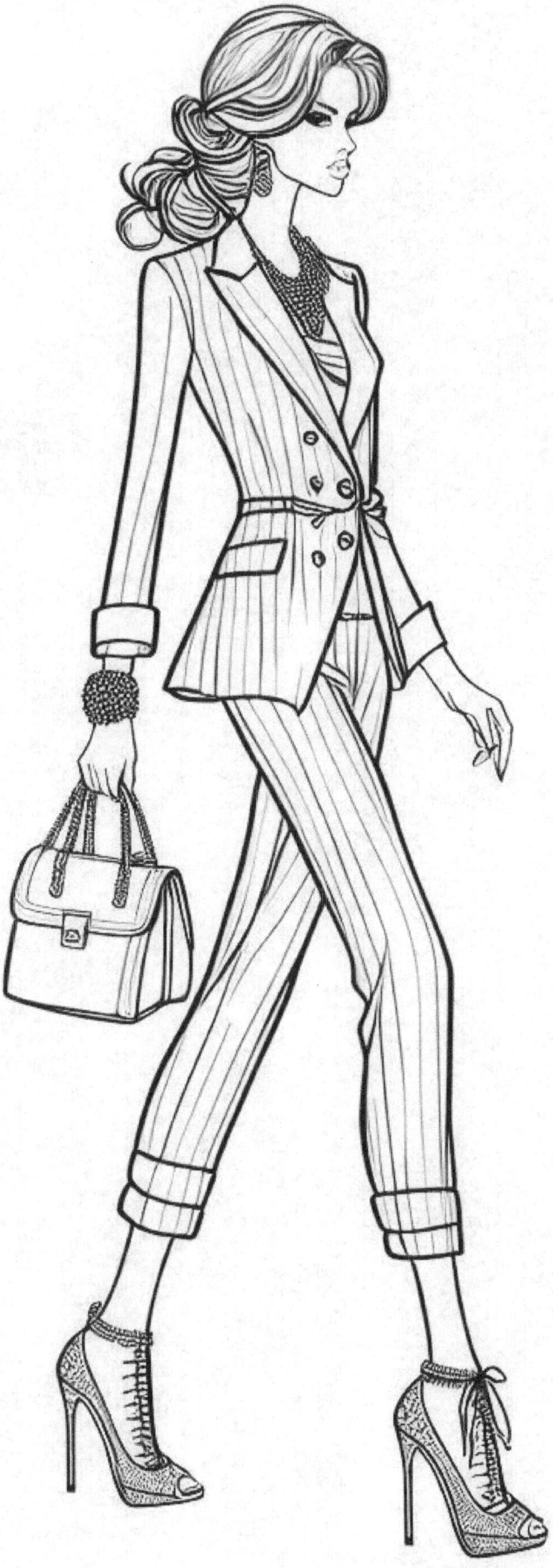

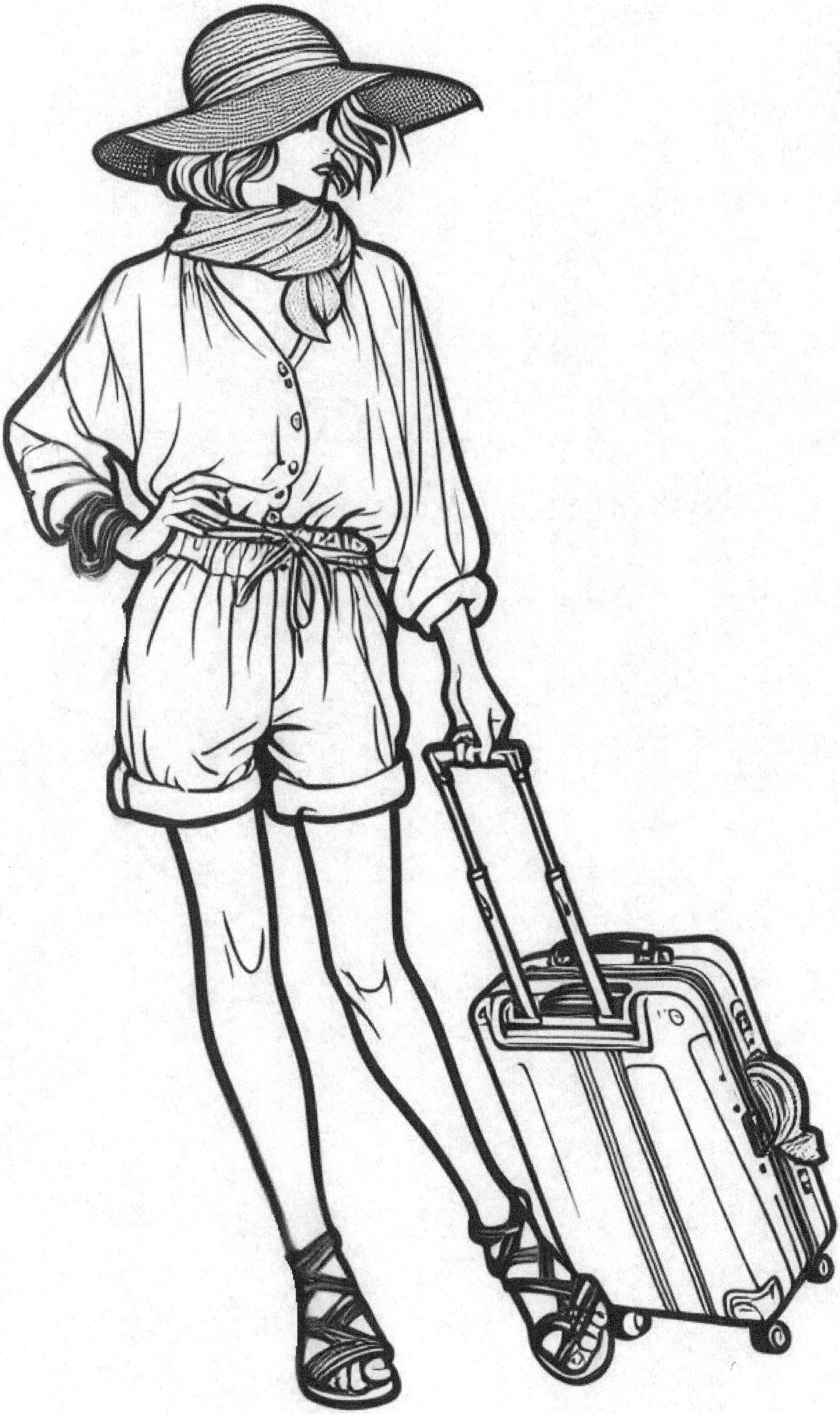

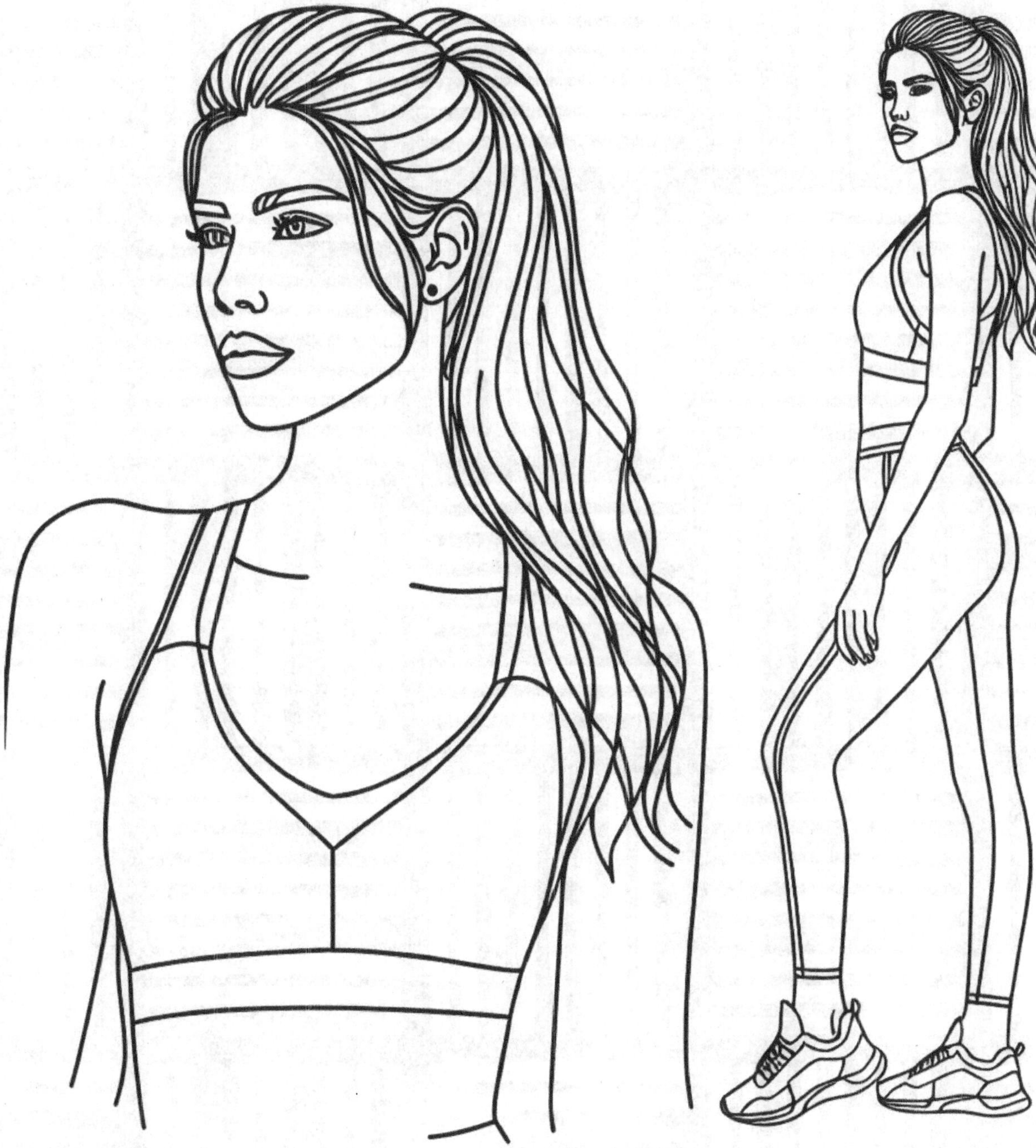

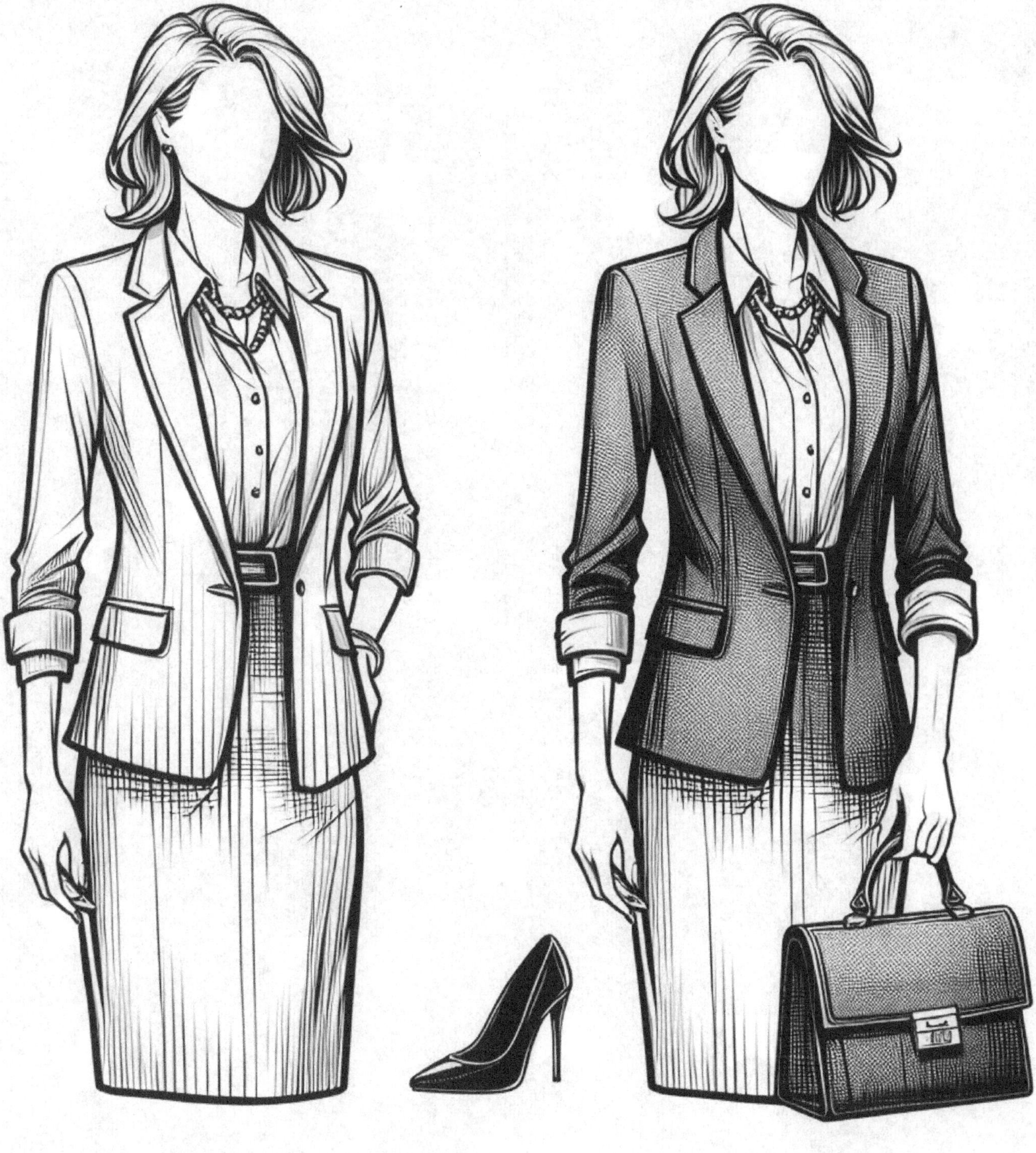

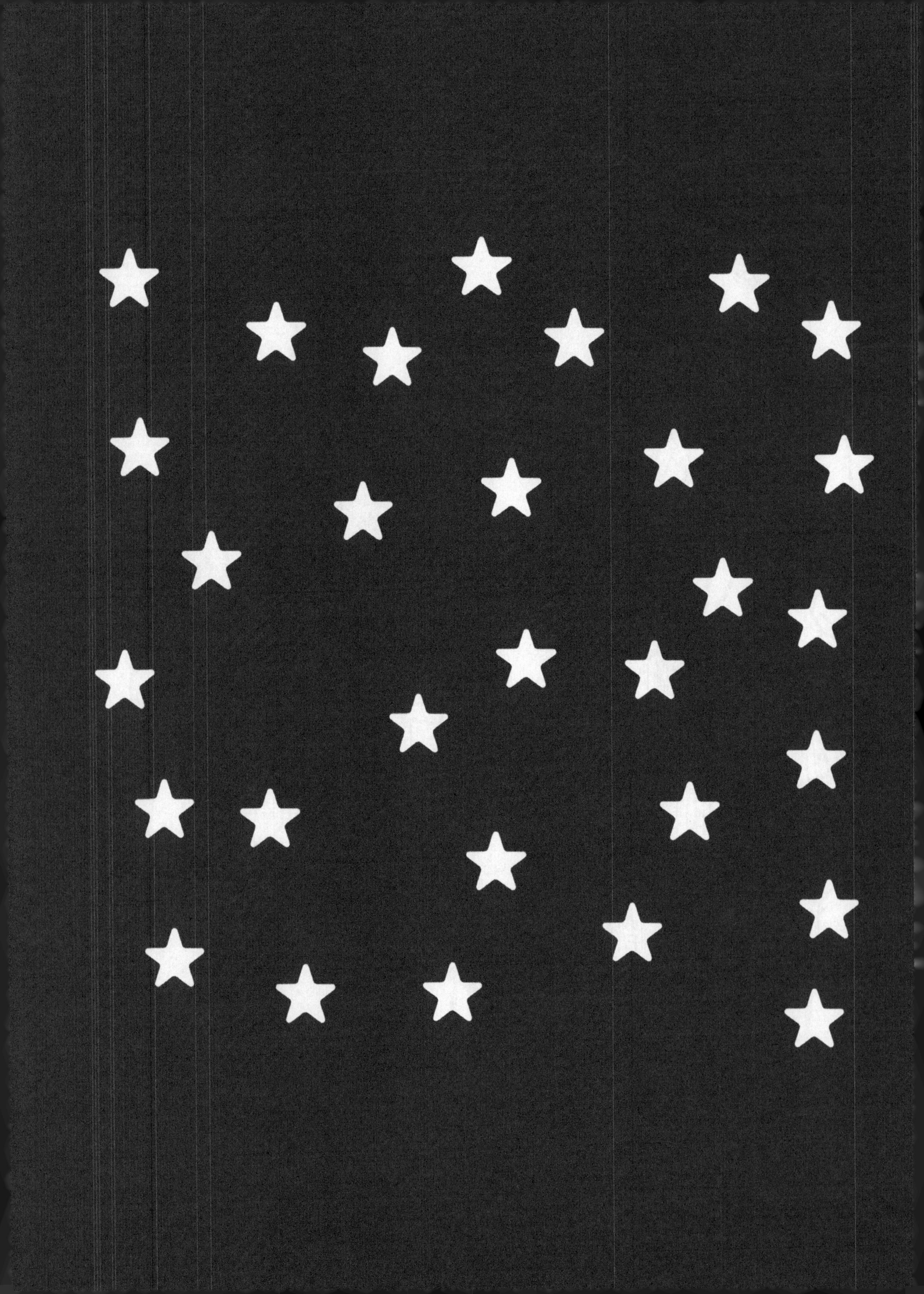

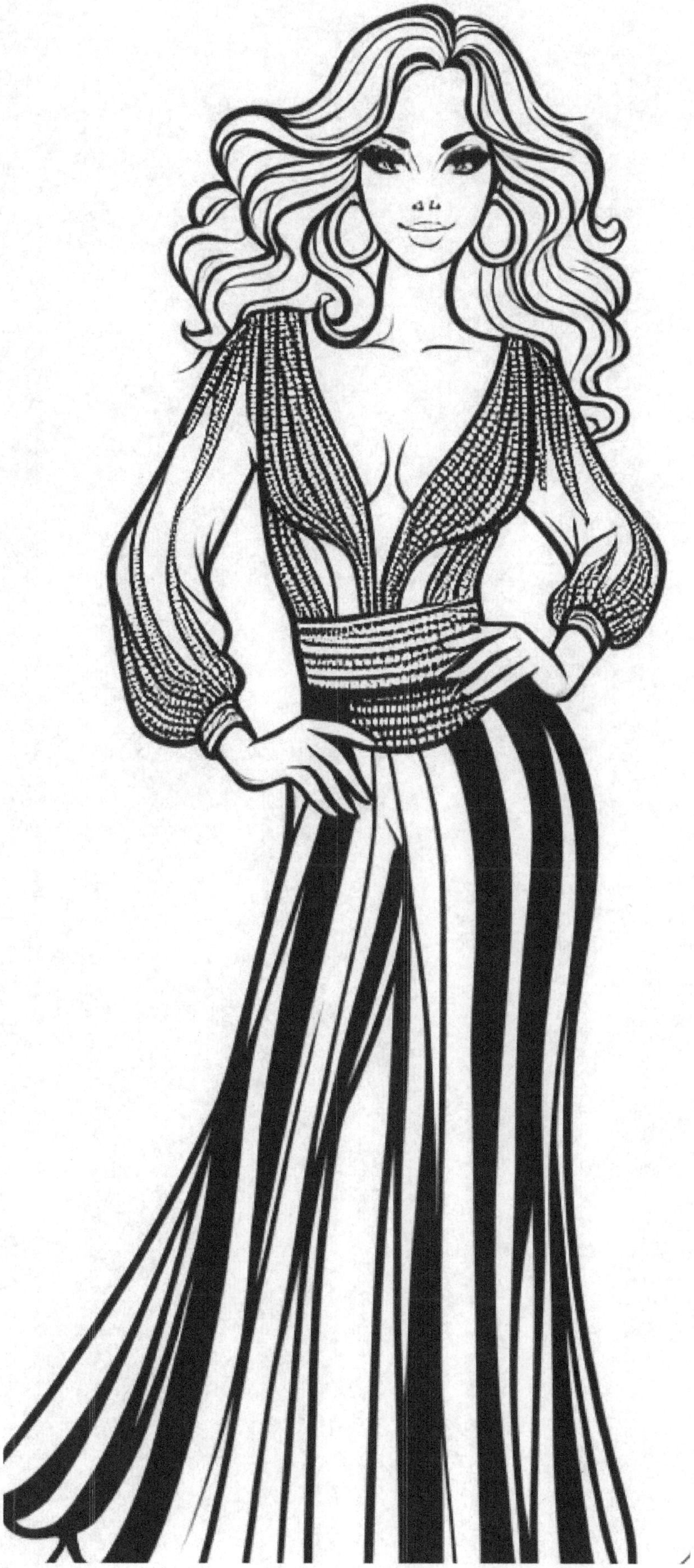

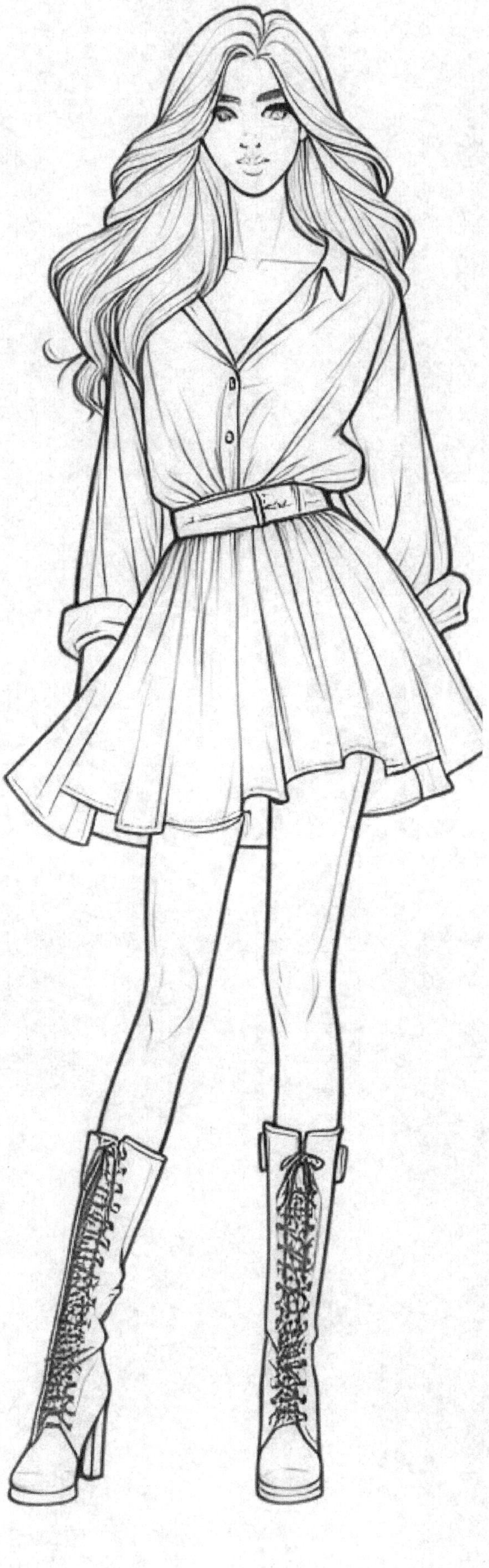

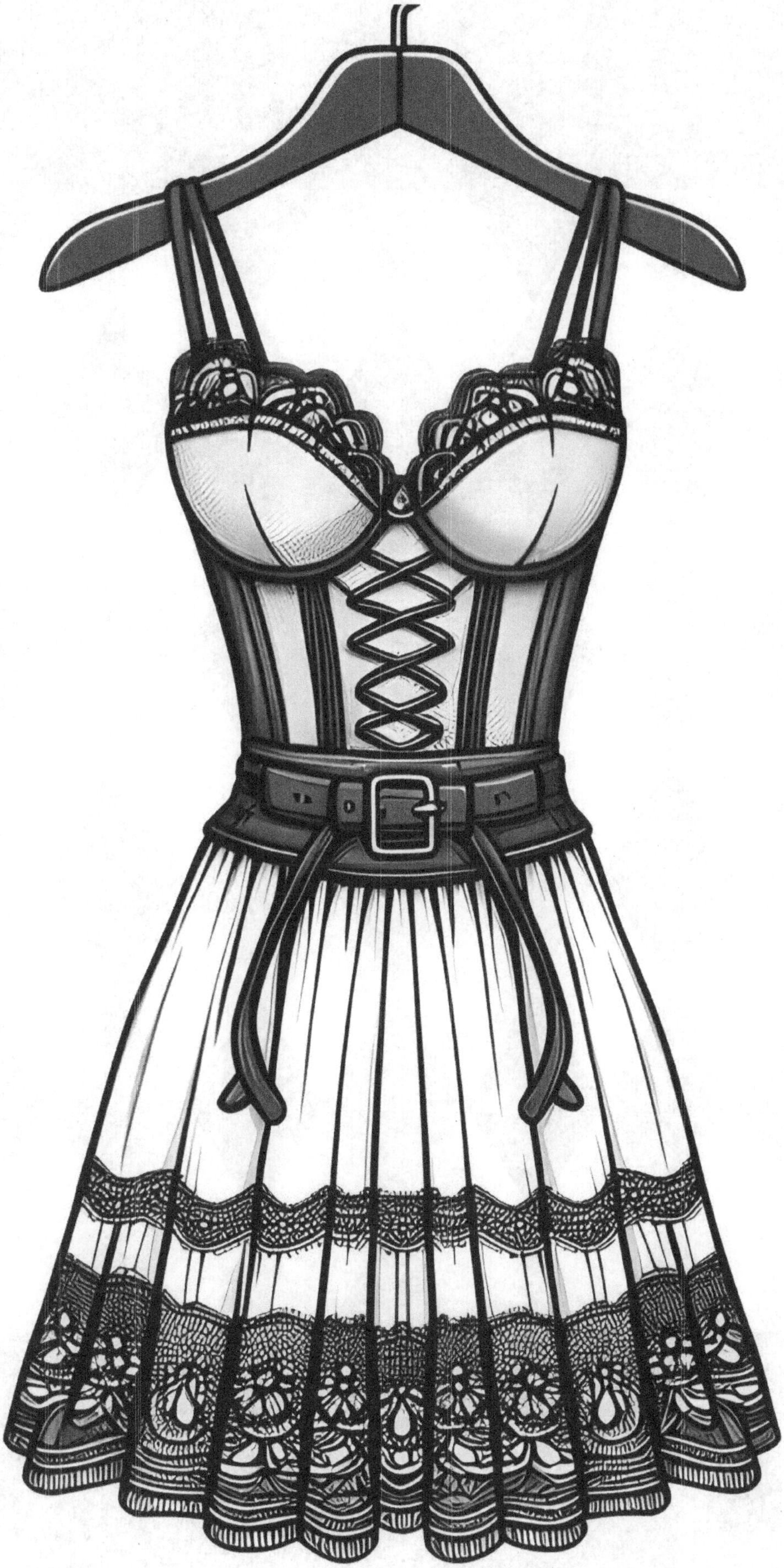

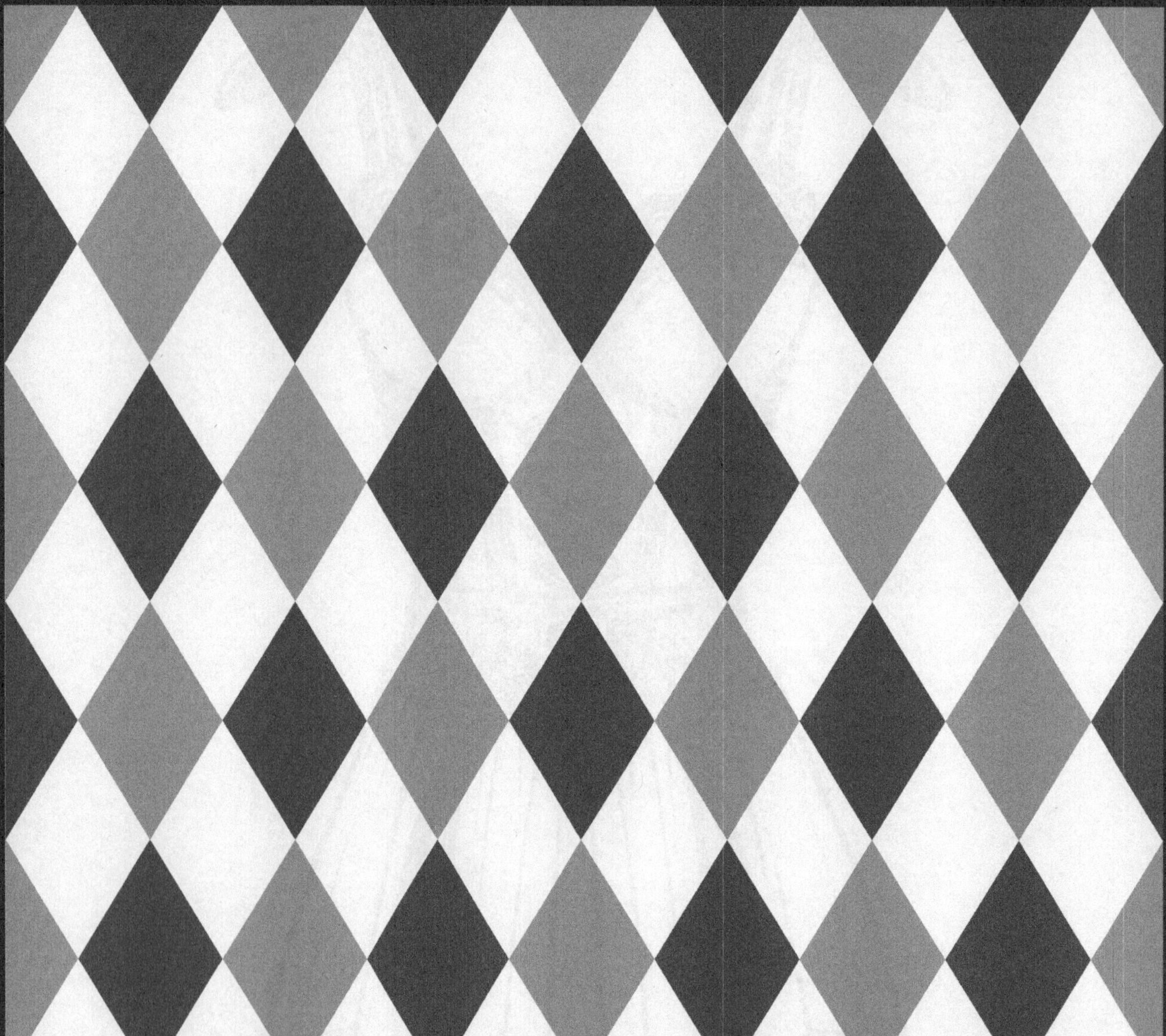

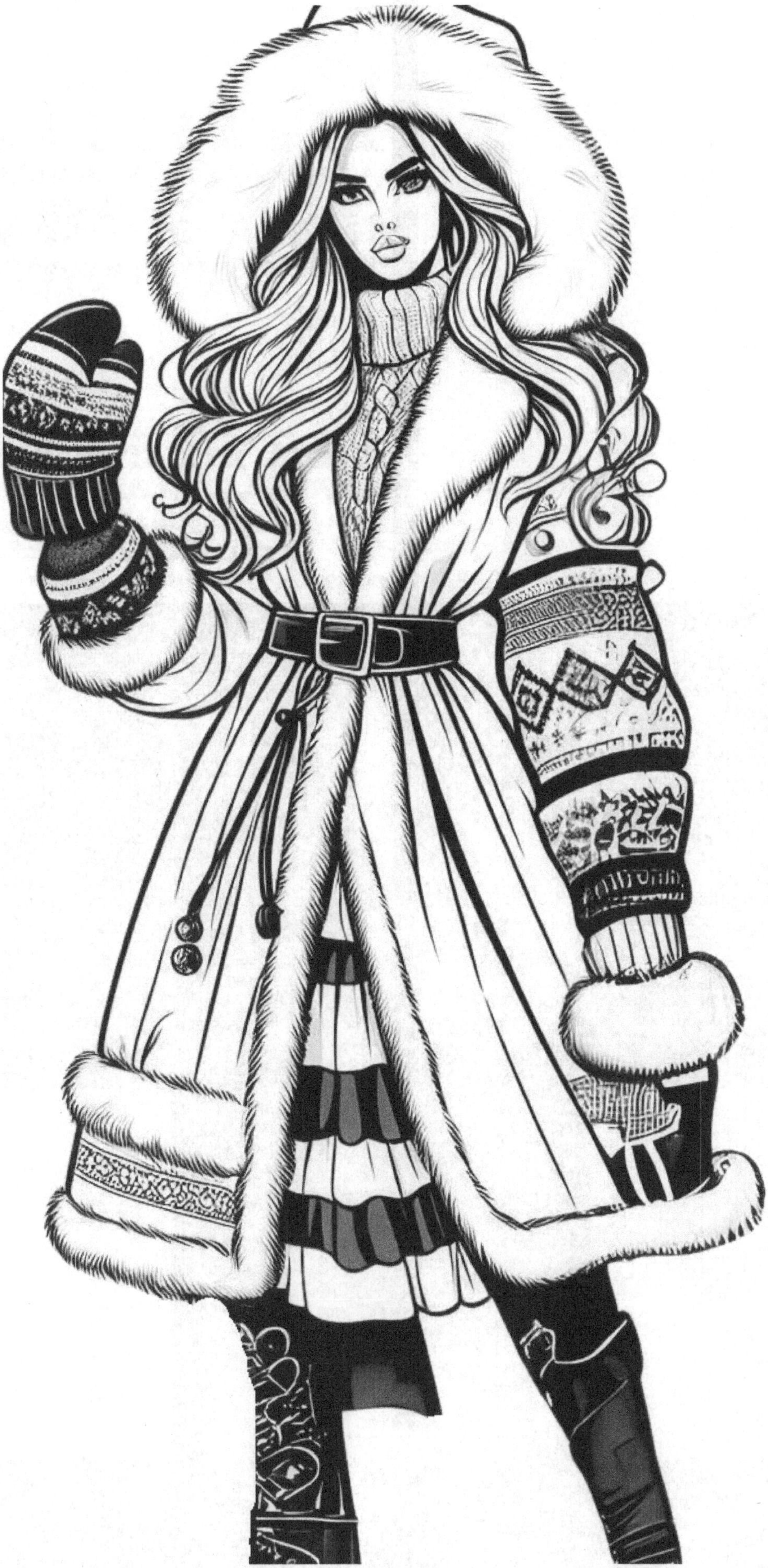

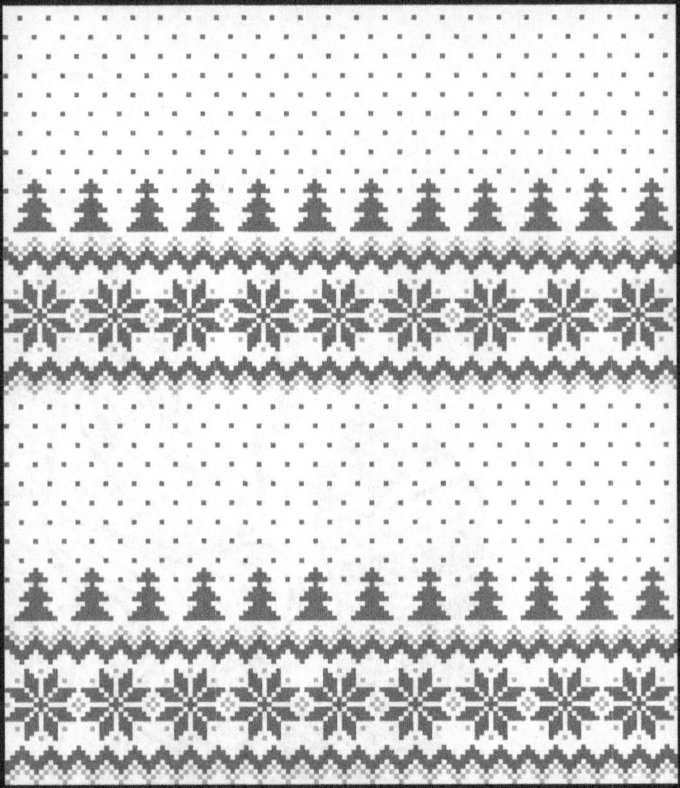
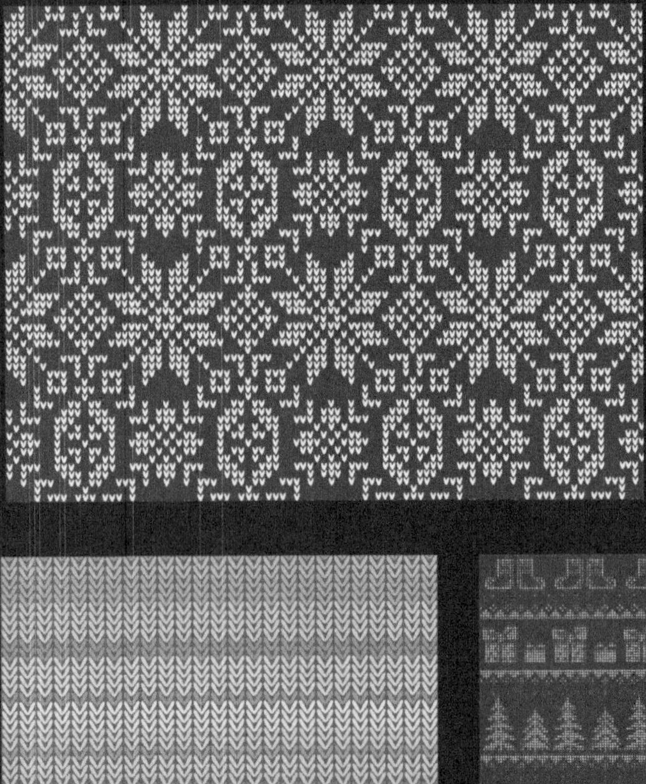
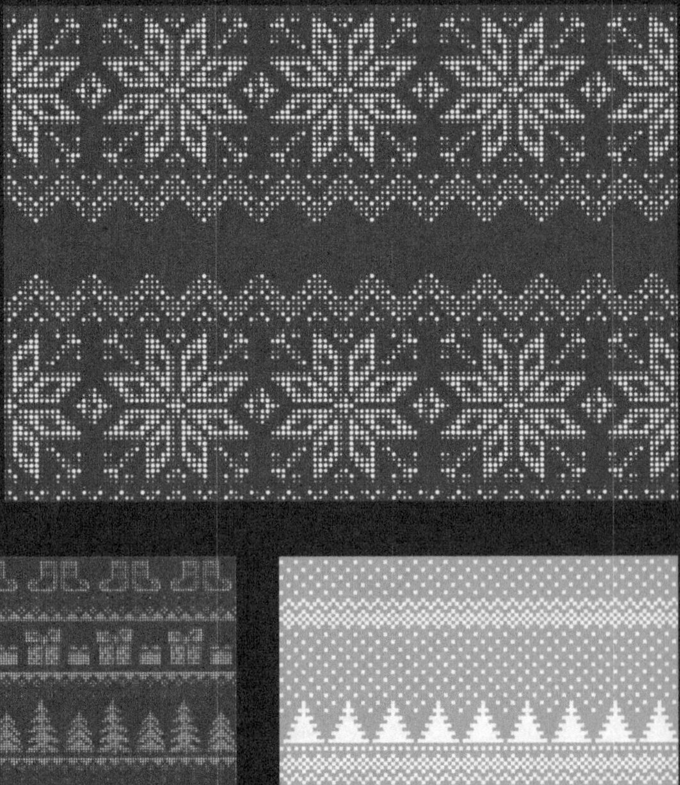
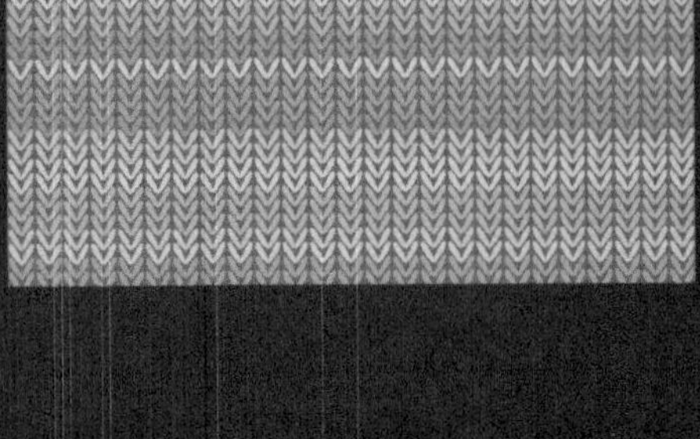

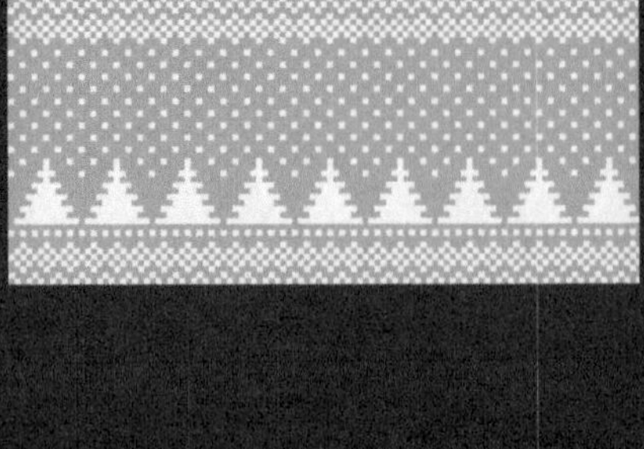

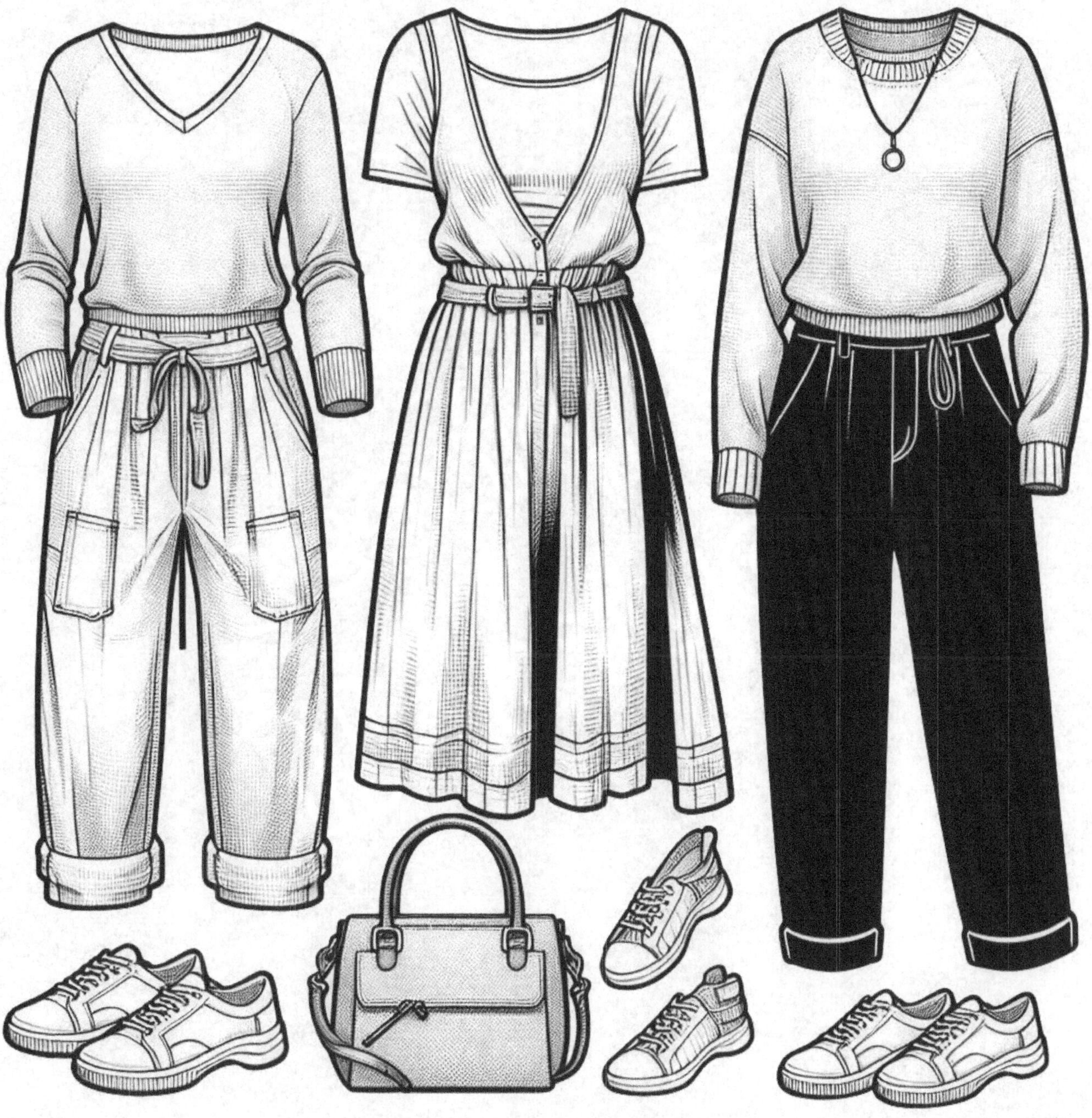

Express yourself

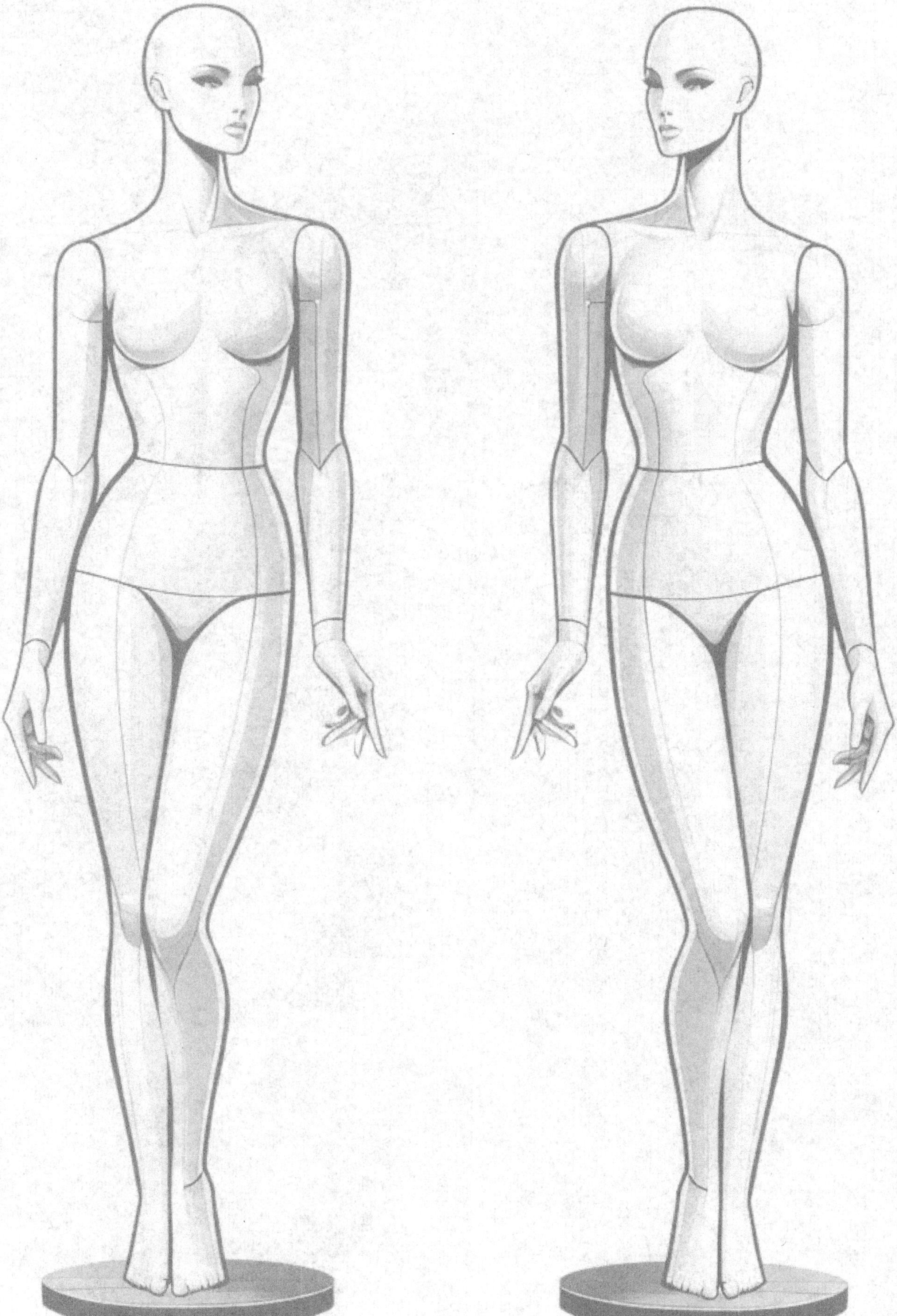

Made in United States
North Haven, CT
10 December 2024

61833992R00043